The Fishes Of East-Greenland

Adolf Severin Jensen

The Fishes of East-Greenland.

By

Ad. S. Jensen.

With three plates.

Reprinted from „MEDDELELSER OM GRÖNLAND" Vol. XXIX.

Copenhagen.

Printed by Bianco Luno.

1904.

When I was requested to give a list of the fishes collected by the Amdrup-expedition of 1898—99 and the Amdrup-Hartz-expedition 1900, I resolved also to take into consideration the material which the Zoological Museum has obtained in other ways up to last autumn, and to compile the notes upon this subject spread in literature or, in other words to give a general survey of the Fish-Fauna of East-Greenland.

My colleagues will perhaps think that the material at hand is not everywhere treated as universally as might be wished. I admit this objection to be justified, but at the same time I must inform them that I am just now preparing a survey of the Fish-Fauna of all Greenland destined for publication in *Conspectus Faunæ Groenlandicæ* and for this reason I have not everywhere entered into minute examinations.

With respect to the position of the localities mentioned in the list, I refer to the splendid maps in volume X and XXVII of „Meddelelser om Grönland", and to the map in the second volume of Professor Nathorst's book „Två Somrar i Norra Ishafvet" (1900). In the present treatise p. 224 will moreover be found a list of the localities drawn up for the greater part by Lieut. C. Amdrup. Where more localities have been recorded they are arranged successively from South to North.

I hereby tender my heartiest thanks to Prof. Dr. F. A. Smitt (Stockholm) and Dr. E. Lönnberg (Upsala) who have kindly given me admission to and information with regard to the fishes collected by the Swedish expeditions to East-Greenland.

Copenhagen, Zoological Museum, jan. 1903.

Ad. S. Jensen.

I have tried to include in this list all the fishes from the East-coast of Greenland which are known up till the present time. It embraces the following species which will be more thoroughly treated in the subjoined pages:

Scorpænidæ.

Sebastes marinus L., p. 225.

Trichiuridæ.

Aphanopus minor Coll., p. 226.

Cottidæ.

Cottunculus microps Coll., p. 226.
Gymnacanthus tricuspis Reinh., p. 227.
Cottus quadricornis L., p. 228.
Cottus scorpius L., p. 239.
Artediellus uncinatus Reinh., p. 241.
Icelus bicornis Reinh., p. 245.
Triglops pingelii Reinh., p. 247.

Gasterosteidæ.

Gasterosteus aculeatus L., p. 248.

Discoboli.

Cyclopterus lumpus L., p. 249.
Cyclopterus (Eumicrotremus) spinosus Müll., p. 250.
Liparis liparis L., p. 251.

Liparis fabricii Kr., p. 252.
Liparis (Careproctus) reinhardti Kr., p. 255.

Blenniidæ.
Lumpenus maculatus Fries, p. 255.
Lumpenus lampetriformis Walb., p. 255.
Lumpenus medius Reinh., p. 256.

Zoarcidæ.
Lycodes pallidus Coll., p. 256.
Lycodes eudipleurostictus Jensen, p. 257.
Lycodes reticulatus Reinh. var. n. *macrocephalus*, p. 258.
Lycodes seminudus Reinh., p. 260.
Lycenchelys kolthoffi n. sp., p. 261.
Gymnelis viridis Fabr., p. 264.

Gadidæ.
Gadus callarias L., p. 265.
Gadus ogac Rich., p. 265.
Gadus saida Lep., p. 266.
Brosmius brosme Ascan., p. 270.
Onus reinhardti (Kr.) Coll., p. 270.

Macruridæ.
Macrurus fabricii Sundev., p. 271.

Pleuronectidæ.
Hippoglossus hippoglossoides Walb., p. 271.
Drepanopsetta (Platysomatichthys) platessoides Fabr., p. 272.

Paralepididæ.
Paralepis kröyeri Lütk., p. 272.

Salmonidæ.
Salmo alpinus L., p. 273.
Mallotus villosus Müll., p. 274.

Plagiostomi.
Somniosus microcephalus Bl. Schn., p. 276.

The number — 36 species altogether — seems small, yet it is not quite inconsiderable when we remember the severe climate of the sea. Moreover we may expect the list to be increased in the course of time. Perhaps not very many «new» species will be added from the north of East-Greenland, as this part of the coast has been visited by several well equipped expeditions, especially of late years. On the other hand a closer examination is still needed with regard to the southern part of the coast from Kap Farewell to the Arctic circle, as only a small part of the latter viz. the neighbourhood of Angmagsalik has been explored, and then only more or less casually, and just here we may as I shall soon explain still expect to make interesting discoveries.

A few universal remarks about the Fish-Fauna of East-Greenland will not be deemed out of place as an introduction to the systematical list.

As will be percieved the deep-sea fishes properly so-called are not mentioned in the list (perhaps with a single exception: *Aphanopus minor* Coll. compare p. 226); very little is indeed as yet known of the abyssal fish-fauna off East-Greenland. I have had the opportunity of seeing at the «Riks-Museum» of Stockholm the ichthyological result of a trawling done by the Kolthoff-expedition in 1900, between Jan Mayen and Greenland (72° 42' lat. N. 14° 49' long. W.) at a depth of 2000 metres: *Lycodes frigidus* Coll., *Paraliparis bathybii* Coll. and *Rhodichthys regina* Coll. All three species are characteristic of the deep icy Polar sea, and are not known elsewhere [1]. In Denmark Strait between Iceland and Greenland some trawling was done by the Danish Ingolf-expedition 1895—96, and here from

---

[1] I have proved in my •Ichthyologiske Studier• (p. 207) (Vidensk. Medd. Naturhist. Foren. Kbhvn. 1901) that the *Lycodes* from the deep Atlantic off the East-coast of North America, which American ichthyologists have identified with the *Lycodes frigidus* Coll. of the Polar sea, is a different species which I have designated *L. atlanticus*.

depths of 568—1300 fathoms (stations 11, 90 and 91) quite different abyssal fishes were brought to light: *Macrurus (Coryphœnoides) rupestris* Gunn., *M. ingolfi* Lütk., *M. (Hymenocephalus) goodei* Günth. and *M. (Chalinura) simulus* G. & B. all of them characteristic of the deep warm Atlantic sea. In these hauls we have an indication that the abyssal fish-fauna of East-Greenland belongs to two different deep-sea faunas, one n o r-t h e r n with the same species of fishes as the rest of the deep Polar sea (this means a deep-sea which is not bounded by the Arctic-circle, but by the submarine ridges of the sea-bottom between Greenland—Iceland—the Faroe Islands and the Shetland Islands), and one s o u t h e r n with the same species of fishes as the large Atlantic-basin. This is of course due to the hydrographical conditions. The said ridges prevent an exchange of the deeper layers of water so that North of the ridges, from the bottom up to about 300 fathoms under the surface, Polar water is constantly found with a temperature below 0° C., and South of the ridges we have Atlantic water the temperature of which is always positive [1]).

The influence of Atlantic water seems also to be traceable nearer East-Greenland at the s o u t h e r n part of the coast. Now and again especially in July and during the end of the summer off the fjords in the neighbourhood of A n g m a g s a l i k (Sermilik a. s. o.) at about 65° 35′ lat. N., the Eskimo harpoon Crested Seals *(Cystophora cristata)* coming to the surface with large fishes in their mouths. In this way the museum has obtained fishes as *Brosmius brosme* Ascan., and *Macrurus rupestris* Sundev., species which live at depths of about 50—300 fathoms, and which as far as I know are not fond of Polar water. I therefore presume that at any rate at some times of the year warm Atlantic water must be found off the coast of

---

[1]) Compare besides my above mentioned treatise in Vidensk. Medd. Naturhist. Foren. Kbhvn. 1901.

Angmagsalik. Species as Rose-fish (*Sebastes marinus* L.) and the Cod (*Gadus callarias* L.) which are only exceptionally found in Polar water are likewise only known from Angmagsalik, and south of this place. Where trawling has been done farther north at corresponding depths only pure Cold-water species have been caught (as *Lycodes eudipleurostictus* Jensen, and *L. pallidus* Coll.) or species which thrive in sea water of both positive (low) and negative degree (as *Cottunculus microps* Coll., and *Liparis (Careproctus) reinhardti* Kr.).

The shallow-water fish-fauna as far as can be judged at present, is arctic, and as will be seen by the list the same species are for the greater part met with all along the long coast-line. *Cottus quadricornis* L. forms however a remarkable exception. It is plentiful enough from Turner Sund and farther north but is not found at Angmagsalik. The circumstance that this high-arctic fish[1]) is not found at the southern coast is interesting considered f. i. in connection with the fact that an equally strongly marked high-arctic species among the Mollusca viz. *Yoldia (Portlandia) arctica* Gray (which lives together with *C. quadricornis* in Turner Sund and farther north) is also missing at the southern part of the coast. On the other hand there is among the Mollusca a boreo-arctic species which thrives admirably at Angmagsalik, but does not appear farther north, viz. the common Mussel (*Mytilus edulis* L.). I do not therefore consider it quite improbable that when the southern coast gets

---

[1]) At West-Greenland it does not go farther south than Baffin Bay; else it lives at the Arctic America, in the Icy sea of Siberia, and in the White-Sea (and in the inner part of the Baltic, and some large lakes connected with this sea, where it is considered as a relict-species from the Glacial-period). It has been found farther north than any other fish viz. at $82^1/2°$ lat. N. (Dumb-bell harbour at Grinnell-Land). — It is not unknown to me that writers as Francis Day maintain its distribution at the British Islands, but I feel convinced that these accounts are based on some mistakes. I also consider as wrongly determined the young ones which have lately been described and figured by English biologists as young ones of •*C. quadricornis*•.

rationally explored there may be found also in the littoral region some comparatively southern fish-species. May not also the circumstance that the Capelan (*Mallotus villosus* Müll.) has not been observed to resort to the coast to spawn, farther north than Angmagsalik (compare p. 275—76), point in the same direction? So much may be said with regard to the littoral fauna that though it is arctic on the whole a degree of difference asserts itself between the southmost and the more northerly coast as the latter is inhabited by certain high-arctic species of animals which are not found at the former part[1]).

The pelagic fish life off East-Greenland is hardly known at all. The frequent occurence of the Polar-cod (*Gadus saida* Lep.) (and other shore-forms) among the field-ice is very interesting (compare p. 267—68).

In the fresh waters of East-Greenland only two species of fishes are found viz. the Threespined Stickleback (*Gasterosteus aculeatus* L. var. *gymnurus* C. V.) and the Arctic Charr (*Salmo alpinus* L.); the last named however lives part of the time in fresh, and part of the time in salt water (compare p. 274).

With respect to a judgment of the quantitative composition of the fish-fauna we have only few data to go by, as only few hauls were made with appliances fit for the catching of fish. Yet it seems as if certain coast-fishes are found in rather large numbers. By a sweep with an eel-seine which the Zoologist Sören Jensen made at Angmagsalik in the middle of September 1900, and where the seine was drawn from 9 fathoms to the shore, no less than 120 fishes were thus caught consisting chiefly of: *Gymnacanthus tricuspis, Cottus scorpius, Icelus bicornis, Triglops pingelii* and *Gadus saida*. Another sweep with eel-seine at Jameson Land in Hurry Inlet (at the

---

[1]) Where the boundary is situated between the zoo-geographical ·southern· and ·northern· coast, cannot be determined at the present time, as the coast from Angmagsalik to Kap Dalton zoologically is practically unexplored.

beginning of August 1900) where the seine was drawn from 7—0 fathoms gave 80 fishes altogether, for the greater part *Gymnacanthus tricuspis*, *Triglops pingelii* and *Gadus saida* (fry) [1].

List of the Literature in which are found communications about Fishes from East-Greenland.

William Scoresby jr.: Journal of a voyage to Northern Whalefishery. Edinburgh 1823.

In the report of this voyage where the East-coast of Greenland was navigated from about 70—75° lat. N. 4 species of fishes met with are mentioned (Appendix No. III, p. 423). One was the Greenland Shark (*Somniosus microcephalus* Bl. Schn.) which is here designated «*Squalus borealis*» [2]. The three others were found in the stomachs of Narwhals: «*Raja batis*» is presumably wrongly determined as to species. «*Gadus carbonarius*(?)» and «*Pleuronectes —?*» can only be determined as to genus.

W. A. Graah: Undersøgelsesrejse til Østkysten af Grønland. Kjøbenhavn 1832.

Lieutenant Graah who explored the southern part of the East-coast of Greenland mentions (p. 194) 8 species of fishes which he himself has seen there. He mentions them partly by Danish and Greenland names, partly by systematical names taken from O. Fabricii Fauna Groenlandica or imparted to him by Professor Reinhardt sen. The species are: *Gymnacanthus tricuspis* Reinh. («Ulke» etc), *Sebastes marinus* L. («Rødfisk» etc.), *Salmo alpinus* L. («Ørred» etc.), *Mallotus villosus* Müll. («Lodde» etc.), *Gadus callarias* L. («Torsk» etc.), *Gadus ogac* Rich. («Torsk», «Ogak» etc.), *Hippoglossus hippoglossoides* Walb. («Helleflynder» etc.), *Somniosus microcephalus* Bl. Schn. («Hajfisk» etc.).

Die zweite Deutsche Nordpolarfahrt in den Jahren 1869 und 1870 unter Führung des Kapitän Karl Koldeway. 2. Bd. Wissenschaftliche Ergebnisse. Leipzig 1874. II. Zoologie.

At page 169—173 Professor W. C. H. Peters mentions 6 species which the above named expedition («The Germania-expedition») brought home from Kap Broer Ruys, and from Jackson-, Clavering-, Sabine- and Shannon Ø. The species are: *Cottus quadricornis* L. («*C. hexacornis* Rich.»), *Cottus*

---

[1] The expedition also carried with them a large Otter-trawl, but faults in the rigging and manœuvring of it brought about that hardly any catch was got by it wherefore it was quite given up after a few attempts, and hereby the opportunity was unfortunately lost for rational deep-water fishing. The Beam-trawl employed instead of the former only gave a very slight yield of fish.

[2] Described and figured by Scoresby in: An account of the Arctic Regions. Vol. I, p. 538, table XV, fig. 3—5.

scorpius L. (•*C. porosus* C. V.•), *Icelus bicornis* Reinh. (•*I. hamatus* Kr.•), *Liparis fabricii* Kr.? (•*L. gelatinosus* Pall.•), *Gadus saida* Lep. (•*G glacialis* Peters n. sp.•), *Salmo alpinus* L. (•?*S. Hoodii* Rich.•).

Robert Collett: **Aphanopus minor**, en ny Dybvandsfisk af Tri-chiuridernes Familie fra Grønland. Christiania Videnskabs-Selskabs Forhandlinger 1886. No. 19.

Description of a new species *Aphanopus* taken off the southern part of East-Greenland.

Den østgrønlandske Expedition, udført i Aarene 1883—85 un-der Ledelse af G. Holm. 2. Del. Meddelelser om Grønland. 10. Hefte. Kjøbenhavn 1888.

Captain G. Holm mentions (p. 54) of the fishes which are found at Angmagsalik at the southern part of East-Greenland: •Angmagsæt'er• (*Mallotus villosus* Müll.), •Hajer• '(*Somniosus microcephalus* Bl. Schn.), •Lax• (*Salmo alpinus* L.), •Ulke•, •Stenbidere• (*Cyclopterus*), •Rødfisk• (*Sebastes marinus* L.), •Fjordtorsk• (*Gadus ogac* Rich.), •Helleflyndere• (*Hippoglossus hippoglossoides* Walb.). At page 81—82 he gives some interesting informa-tion about the food-fishes which are of importance for the Eskimo: Sharks, Salmon and Angmagsæt.

F. A. Smitt: Skandinaviens Fiskar. 1. Del. Stockholm 1892.

At page 159 is mentioned a *Cottunculus microps* Coll., taken off the South-eastern part of Greenland by the Nordenskiöld-expedition 1883.

Den østgrønlandske Expedition, udført i Aarene 1891—92 un-der Ledelse af C. Ryder. Meddelelser om Grønland. 19. Hefte. 1896.

E. Bay, who was the zoologist of this expedition, gives a report, p 52—58, of the fishes caught or observed especially from Scoresby Sund and Angmagsalik. The determinations as to species are by C. F. Lütken. Altogether 15 species are mentioned viz.: *Cottus quadricornis* L., *Cottus scorpius* L., *Gymnacanthus tricuspis* Reinh. (•*Phobetor ventralis* C. V.•), *Artediellus* (•*Centridermichthys*•) *uncinatus* Reinh., *Icelus bicornis* Reinh. (•*I. hamatus* Kr.•), *Cyclopterus spinosus* Fabr., *Liparis fabricii* (•*L.* sp.•\), *Lumpenus lampetriformis* Walb., *Gymnelis viridis* Fabr., *Gasterosteus aculeatus* L., *Gadus saida* Lep., *Salmo alpinus* L., *Mallotus villosus* Müll., *Paralepis kröyeri* Lütk., *Somniosus microcephalus* Bl. Schn. — It more-over contains biological observations of some of the species.

F. A. Smitt: On the genus *Lycodes*. Bihang till K. Svenska Vet. Akad. Handlingar. Bd. 27. Afd. IV. No. 4. Stockholm 1901.

This treatise contains among other things descriptions of the *Lycodinæ* caught by the Nathorst-expedition 1899, and the Kolthoff-expedition 1900, at the northern part of East-Greenland (Franz Joseph's Fjord and farther north). Through the kindness of Professor Smitt, I have had the opportunity of examining this material and have thereby arrived at the result that it contains the following species from East-Greenland: *Lycodes pallidus* Coll., *L. eudipleurostictus* Jensen, *L. reticulatus* Reinh. var. n. *macrocephalus*, *L. seminudus* Reinh. and *Lycenchelys kolthoffi* n. sp.

E. Lønnberg: The fishes of the Swedish zoological polar expedition of 1900. Revue internationale de pêche et de pisciculture. Vol. II, No. 4. St.-Pétersbourg 1900.

Gives a list of the fishes which were caught by the Kolthoff-expedition 1900, at the North-eastern part of Greenland, containing, besides the above mentioned *Lycodinæ* which are partly designated by other names, 12 species whereof *Triglops pingelii* Reinh., *Liparis (Careproctus) reinhardti* Kr. (*Cyclogaster gelatinosus*) and *Drepanopsetta platessoides* Fabr. were new to the fauna of East-Greenland. Dr. Lønnberg kindly imparted to me, for use in this treatise, information with regard to some of the rarer species.

———

During the last years some rather considerable collections have moreover been made by Danes at East-Greenland. The ichthyological results of these collections will be mentioned for the first time in this treatise. We are indebted for new contributions to the following gentlemen:

Cand. med. & chir. K. Poulsen who was a member of Lieutenant Amdrup's expedition 1898—99, brought home from Angmagsalik and some places north of it 10 species of fishes of which *Liparis liparis* L. was new to the fauna.

The late Mag. sc. Sören Jensen who was the zoologist of the Amdrup-Hartz-expedition 1900 brought home a very considerable material of fishes, from a quantitative point of view, taken at the tract from Sabine Ø to Angmagsalik [1]). The collection contained 15 species of which *Lumpenus medius* Reinh. was new to the fauna. This collection is of great importance because we can thereby judge of the relative frequency of some species (compare p. 214—15). A diary left by Jensen contained among other things some biological notes about fishes from which some extracts are found in this treatise.

Johan Petersen, commercial manager, and Søren Nielsen, assistant, at Angmagsalik, sent us respectively in 1900 and 1901 7 species of fishes whereof *Brosmius brosme* Ascan. was new to the fauna.

Mag. sc. Chr. Kruuse, who stayed at Angmagsalik 1901—02, for the purpose of botanical studies, took the opportunity at my request of collecting zoologically as well. He brought home 16 species of fishes, whereof no less than 3 were unknown to the fauna of East-Greenland viz.: *Lumpenus maculatus* B. Fries, *Onus reinhardti* (Kr.) Coll. and *Macrurus fabricii* Sundev., and about others we had up till then only verbal records. I am moreover indebted to Kruuse for much information about the fish life at Angmagsalik.

———

[1]) On the way the expedition called at **Jan Mayen**, where however only the following fishes were taken (June 25—28): *Cottus scorpius* L., 1 specimen (depth: 15 fathoms); *Icelus bicornis* Reinh., 9 specimens (depth: 50—60 fathoms); *Lumpenus maculatus* B. Fries, 1 specimen (depth: 50—60 fathoms).

The position of the localities mentioned in the treatise.

	Lat. N.	Long. W.
Amitsuarsik	65° 37′	37° 22′
Angmagsalik	65° 30′—65° 40′	37° 30′—37° 40′
Angmagsalik, off (140 fms.)	65° 30′	37° 20′
Angmagsivik (Kingak)	65° 58′	37° 2′
Danmark Ö	70° 27′	26° 12′
Fleming Inlet (118 fms.)	71° 51′	22° 27′
Forsblads Fjord (3—14 fms.)	72° 28′	25° 23′
Forsblads Fjord (50 fms.)	72° 27′	25° 10′
Forsblads Fjord (90—50 fms.)	72° 27′	25° 28′
Gaaseland	70° 5′—70° 30′	
Hekla Havn	70° 27′	26° 12′
Henry Land, off (20 fms.)	69° 34′	23° 35′
Hurry Inlet (0—3 fms.)	70° 50′.2	22° 31′
Hurry Inlet (0—7 fms.)	70° 50′.2	22° 31′
Hurry Inlet (50 fms.)	70° 36′	22° 31′
Ikerasausak	65° 58′.5	37° 27′
Kangerdlugsuatsiak	66° 18′	35° 28′
Kap Borlase Warren	74° 20′	19°
Kap Broer Ruys	73° 30′	20° 20′
Kap Dan	65° 32′	37°
Kap Hope (120 fms.)	70° 26′	22° 29′
Kap Stewart (6—3 fms.)	70° 25′	22° 37′
Kap Tobin (57 fms.)	70° 23′	22°
Kingorsuak	66° 8′	37° 10′
Römers Fjord (120 fms.)	69° 38′	23° 31′
Sabine Ö (12. 7. 1900)	74° 30′	19° 45′
Sabine Ö, off (18. 7. 1891)	74° 17′	15° 20′
Sabine Ö, SE. of (10. 7. 1900)	74° 25′	18° 30′
Sierak	65° 57′	37° 5′
Tasiusak	65° 37′	37° 34′
Tiningnekelak	65° 56′	37° 40′
Turner Sund (0—2 fms.)	69° 44′	23° 29′.5
Turner Sund (3 fms.)	69° 44′	23° 30′
Turner Sund (8 fms.)	69° 43′.5	23° 33′
Ödesund	66° 15′	35° 25′

Scorpænidæ.

Sebastes marinus Linné.

Off Tasiusak. Drifting among the ice. 26. 8. 1899.
1 specim. 91 mm.

Off Angmagsalik. 140 fms. 18. 9. 1900. Trawl. 1 specim.
About 190 mm.

Sermilik at Angmagsalik. 1901. 1 specim. About 200 mm.

The numbers of the rays in the fins of these three specimens are: D. 15 + 14 — 15. A. 3 + 8 — 9. P. 19. V. 1 + 5.

G. Holm (l. c. p. 54) mentions the Rose-fish among the fish eaten by the inhabitants of Angmagsalik, but they only get it when the Crested-Seal (*Cystophora cristata* Erxl.) brings it to the surface, they do not catch it themselves, of course because they are not acquainted with hook-fishing, and the rose-fish is, as is well known, a deep-sea fish.

Sören Jensen brought home a lot of young ones about 25—30 mm. long, caught by the Greenlanders at the «Angmag-sæt»-station at Angmagsalik. They were arranged in a long row, with heads alternating, drawn on a string, and rolled up into a bundle with a string tied round it. Jensen told me that such bundles serve as toys for the Greenland-children. Holm therefore presumably refers to the young ones of *S. marinus* when he writes (l. c. p. 82): «Some quite small fishes called *iterdlarnat* are treated in the same way (viz. as the Angmagsæt [*Mallotus villosus* Müll.]), but presumably only for diversion.» [1]

---

[1] During the printing of this, I was informed by Commander G. Holm that a roll of «iterdlarnat» had been presented by him to our Ethnographical Museum. The director of the said Museum allowed me kindly to examine this roll, and it turned out to be made up just of the *Sebastes marinus*-fry, of the same size, and handled in the same way as that already mentioned.

Fry of *S. marinus* is thus found in great numbers at Angmagsalik, at any rate at the time (last part of May and June), when the «Angmagsæt» seek in to deposit their spawn.

Trichiuridæ.

Aphanopus minor Collett.

1886. *Aphanopus minor* Collett, Christiania Vidensk.-Selsk. Forhandl. 1886, No. 19.

One specimen of this Trichiurid — the only one known up till this time — was got July 4th 1886 off the southern East-coast of Greenland (65° lat. N., 31° long. W.). It was still alive when it was taken out of the water, washed or forced up to the surface by submarine currents together with some *Sebastes marinus* which were likewise in a half dead condition. — It is described by Collett in the place stated, and is kept at the University-Museum of Christiania.

Cottidæ.

Cottunculus microps Collett.

A male specimen, the length of which was 157 mm., was taken on September 6th 1883, by the Nordenskiöld-expedition off the South-eastern Greenland (65° 30′ lat. N.), where the depth was 130 fathoms (F. A. Smitt l. c. p. 159).

E. Lönnberg (l. c. p. 13) mentions it amongst the fishes which were taken by the Kolthoff-expedition 1900 at the North-eastern Greenland, and he communicated to me by letter that it was taken at the mouth of Franz Joseph's Fjord, at a depth of 200—300 metres, and that only one specimen was caught.

Gymnacanthus tricuspis Reinhardt.

Tasiusak. In the harbour in quite shallow water. 1901—1902. 13 specim.

Angmagsalik. At the ice-foot. 1 fm. 31. 5. 1899. 3 specim.

Angmagsalik. July 1899. 2 specim.

Angmagsalik. 10—0 fms. 15—16. 9. 1900. Eel-seine. 13 specim.

Tiningnekelak. 5—10 fms. 18. 9. 1901. 7 specim.

Hekla Havn. About 6 fms. Aug. 1891. Line. 2 specim.

Kap Stewart. 6—3 fms. 21. 8. 1900. Eel-seine. 13 specim.

Hurry Inlet. 7—0 fms. 7—8. 8. 1900. Eel-seine. 55 specim.

Forsblads Fjord, the mouth. 14—3 fms. 28. 8. 1900. Eel-seine. 5 specim.

Kap Broer Ruys. Very shallow water near the beach. 20. 7. 1891. 1 specim.

Sabine Ö. 5—3 fms. 12. 7. 1900. Dredge. 1 specim.

Lönnberg (l. c. p. 13) mentions it amongst the fishes which the Kolthoff-expedition took 1900, by the North-eastern Greenland.

The females are as usual more numerously represented than the males, though not very strikingly so, thus out of the 55 specimens from Hurry Inlet 31 are females, 24 males. The largest female measures 217 mm., the largest male 185 mm.

A young one of this fish is mentioned p. 238—39 and illustrated fig. 6, pl. XI.

Note. The here mentioned species is generally designated *Gymnacanthus (Phobetor) ventralis* Cuv. Val.; but that the last named is identical with *Gymnacanthus pistilliger* Pallas, is suggested both by text and figure of Cuvier-Valenciennes (Hist. Nat. Poiss. IV, 1829, p. 194; Pl. 79, Fig. 1) as well as by its habitat (Kamtschatka); therefore Reinhardt's designation *G. tricuspis* must have the preference. The honour of having restored *G. pistilliger* Pall. as an independent species after Lütken had tried to prove that it was founded on a mistake, is due to F. A. Smitt (Skandinaviens Fiskar I, 1892, p. 161).

Cottus quadricornis Linné.

Turner Sund. 2—0 fms. 25. 7. 1900. Eel-seine. 3 specim.

Hekla Havn. 3—6 fms. 20. 8. 1891. Dredge. 1 specim.

Hurry Inlet, the south coast of Jameson Land. Just near the beach, in very shallow water. 3. 8. 1891. 4 specim. (Fry).

Hurry Inlet. Near the inmost part of the fjord. 3—0 fms. 3. 8. 1900. Eel-seine. 7 specim.

Hurry Inlet. In pools on the beach. 7. 8. 1900. 7 specim. (Fry).

Hurry Inlet. Near the coast. 1. 8. 1900. Eel-seine. 1 specim.

Hurry Inlet. 7—0 fms. 7—8. 8. 1900. Seine. 3 specim.

Sabine Ö. 5—3 fms. 12. 7. 1900. Dredge. 1 specim.

Three specimens were taken by the second German polar-expedition at Kap Broer Ruys, on July 15th 1870.

Lönnberg (l. c. p. 13) mentions it amongst the fishes taken by the Kolthoff-expedition 1900 at the North-eastern Greenland.

Prof. W. Peters, who examined the specimens of the Germania-expedition classed them among *Cottus hexacornis* Richardson [1]) which he however regards as being closely related to *C. quadricornis* L. of the Baltic [2]). He says about this matter: «Verglichen mit einem Exemplar von *C. quadricornis* L. haben die vorliegenden Exemplare etwas kürzere Oberkiefer und die Interorbitalgegend mehr vertieft. Auch ist die Flossenstrahlenzahl eine verschiedene, indem das grösste

---

[1]) The name is as is well known confusing; Richardson had misunderstood his first notes, and ascribed to the «Bull-head» he had caught at Coppermine, but lost later on, nasal spines of the same nature as the characteristic horns on the front and occiput. Later on he again got some specimens from the same part, and he then found out that they were only *C. quadricornis*.

[2]) Die zweite deutsche Nordpolarfahrt, 2. Bd., 1874, Zoologie, p. 169.

Exemplar von 27 cm. Länge, ganz wie Richardson es von seiner Art angiebt, in der ersten Rückenflosse 7 Stacheln und in der zweiten 13 Strahlen hat. Indessen variirt diese Zahl, indem die beiden andern Exemplare D. 8—14 zeigen, ebenso wie alle drei in der Strahlenzahl der Analflosse von einander abweichen, da dieselbe bei dem grössten Exemplare 14, und bei den andern beiden 13 und 15 beträgt.»

Professor Lütken again brought up the question in the first part of his meritorious «Korte Bidrag til nordisk Ichthyographi» [1]. *C. hexacornis* Rich. from .the arctic America he considers to be no other than *C. quadricornis* L., and after having examined one of the specimens from the Germania-expedition and having compared it with specimens of *C. quadricornis* from the Baltic, he could find no difference except that the front of the East-Greenland Fourhorned Bullhead is more concave than the front of the Baltic one [2], but this difference L. does not consider to be of any great importance: «*C. hexacornis* Peters» from East-Greenland is the very same species as the genuine *C. quadricornis* L.

The abundant material brought home by the Amdrup-expedition invites us to a renewed comparison. I have therefore taken a series of measurements of the 16 specimens at hand together with 6 specimens in our Museum from the Baltic (and the lake Vettern) [3].

From these measurements we see that the head in the Baltic form is comparatively a little larger and has longer jaws. The length of the head amounts indeed

---

[1] Foreløbige Meddelelser om nordiske Ulkefiske. Vidensk. Medd. Naturhist. Foren. Kbhvn. 1876 (p. 375).

[2] Jordan and Evermann have been so unfortunate as to quote Lütken's words in such a manner that the fact is reversed (Fishes of North and Middle America II, 1898, p. 2001).

[3] Vettern, 1 specim. (138 mm.); •Central-Sweden• 2 specim. (♀ 178 mm.; ♂ 246 mm.); the gulf of Bothnia, 2 specim. (♂ 208 mm., ♀ 242 mm.); the Baltic by Stockholm (♀ 230 mm.).

in the East-Greenland specimens to 26.6—28.8 % of the total length, the length of the upper jaw to 9.7—11.7 %, and the length of the lower jaw to 12.5—14.6 %; in the specimens from the Baltic the length of the head amounts to 29—33.5 %, the length of the upper jaw to 11.7—14.3 %, and the length of the lower jaw to 15.6—16.9 %. Professor F. A. Smitt has in his work: Skandinaviens Fiskar (I, 1892, p. 177) given some measurements of 11 *C. quadricornis* from the Baltic and Vettern, whereby the limits for variation are certainly somewhat extended, but the total impression remains about the same. In these 11 specimens (total length 73—274 mm.) the length of the head amounts namely to 28.2—33.2 %, the length of the upper jaw to 10.9—15.3 % and the length of the lower jaw to 14.8—17.5 %. Moreover I find that the tail in the specimens at my disposal from the Baltic is a little less slender; of the total length the minimum height of the tail in 8 adult specimens (179—249 mm.) from East-Greenland amounts namely to 3.8—3.9 %, but in 5 adult specimens (178—246 mm.) from the Baltic to 4—4.2 % [1]).

Thus the East-Greenland form has not only a shorter upper jaw than the Baltic form, as pointed out by Professor Peters, but also the lower jaw and the whole head are shorter, and moreover the caudal peduncle is lower, at any rate judged by the material at my disposal. But in all other ways they are perfectly in accordance as far as I can see. Also the numbers of rays which Peters considers to be of some importance nearly

---

[1]) According to the measurements of Professor Smitt, the minimum height of the tail amounts, in 6 adult specimens (173—272 mm.) from the Baltic and Vettern, to 3.8—4.1 % of the total length, a fact which substantially confirms the correctness of the above stated. On the contrary in a seventh specimen (274 mm.) the percentage was stated to be only 3.6 %, but I almost imagine this to be due to a misprint, as S. remarks that in two specimens from the Arctic Sea of Siberia the percentages for the minimum height of the tail, stated to be 3.5—3.6 % of the total length, are low compared with the ones in the specimens from the Baltic.

coincide. According to Lilljeborg [1]) the numbers in Swedish specimens are: $D.^1$ 7—9; $D.^2$ 13—15; A. 14—15; P. 16—17; V. 1 + 3; in the 16 specimens at my disposal from East-Greenland the numbers are: $D.^1$ 7—9; $D.^2$ 13—15; A. 13—15; P. (15) 16; V. 1 + 3; in the 3 specimens from the Germania-expedition: $D.^1$ 7—8; $D.^2$ 13—14; A. 13—15. I do not think either that the front between the eyes is more concave than in the East-Greenland form; the difference is at any rate slight and by no means invariable.

According to my opinion we are not justified in regarding the Fourhorned Bullhead from East-Greenland and the Baltic one as two different species. I do not wish at present to answer the question if we should regard them as special varieties on account of the above named dissimilarities. For in order to decide the question of formation of race, within the present species, it would be necessary to have for comparison specimens from the other places of the habitat of the species, namely from the White-Sea, the Icy Sea of Siberia, and Arctic America, but from these seas I have no material.

I must here however mention that Jordan and Evermann still maintain the species *Cottus (Oncocottus) hexacornis* Richardson, with a western (American-West-Greenland) distribution against *C. (O.) quadricornis* L., with an eastern (European-East-Greenland) distribution, yet remarking that the distinguishing characters between them are of doubtful value, and that they must probably be reduced to one species [2]). In their analytical table the two species are distinguished in the following way:

a. Atlantic species; maxillary short; pectoral moderate; caudal rounded.................................*Quadricornis*

aa. Arctic American species; maxillary longer; pectoral longer; caudal truncate.............................*Hexacornis*

---

[1]) Sveriges och Norges Fiskar, I, 1891, p. 144.
[2]) Fishes of North and Middle America, Part II, 1898, p. 2001—2004.

The here indicated variations are partly more precisely defined in the diagnosis. It is thus said about *C. quadricornis:* «Maxillary reaching to below posterior margin of eye», and about *C. hexacornis*: «Maxillary reaching past the orbit». But in the specimens of *C. quadricornis* I have before me from the Baltic the maxillary just reaches past the orbit, and Lillje-borg[1] likewise says: «Maxillary reaches slightly behind the posterior border of the orbit», so here some mistake must have occurred with regard to the American writers' judgment of the European form. But as J. and E. associate the European and the East-Greenland form probably initiated by Lütken (compare p. 229), there is perhaps some truth in their statement; for as the upper jaw is shorter in the East-Greenland form than in the Baltic one, and as a rule only reaches to below the posterior margin of the eye, its upper jaw is probably also shorter than in the American form. — Moreover is said about the pectoral fins with regard to *C. quadricornis*: «reaching anal», and with regard to *C. hexacornis*: «scarcely reaching front of second dorsal». I cannot however find any distinct difference in these expressions, as the mentioned points in the Cottoid in question lie very near each other in the same perpendicular line. It must besides be taken into consideration that the length of the pectoral fins varies according to sex, and can consequently only with reservation be employed as specific character. In 5 specimens of *C. quadricornis* from the Baltic, which are at my disposal, the pectoral fins of the females reach the anus, or at the utmost to the beginning of the anal fin, but in the males to the beginning of the anal fin or somewhat past it. The variation is still greater in 8 specimens from East-Greenland, as in 3 females the pectoral fins scarcely reach to the end of the first dorsal fin and to the anus, while in 5 males it reaches from the anus and a little past the front part of the anal fin. — Finally with

---

[1] l. c.

respect to the third character that the caudal fin should be «rounded» in *C. quadricornis*, and «truncated with rather sharp corners» in *C. hexacornis*, this does not hold good with regard to *C. quadricornis*. In the specimens before me from the Baltic, the upper and, or, lower rays reach farthest when the caudal fin is folded together, and when it is distended it is truncate, or at any rate only very slightly rounded, the upper corner generally pointed, the lower rounded; this also agrees with Lilljeborg's description: «The caudal fin which is cut off straightly, or flatly curved, sometimes with pointed, sometimes with rounded corners»[1]. There is also some variation in the East-Greenland specimens, as the caudal fin generally is slightly rounded[2]), but often very insignificantly so, nay in one specimen it is even truncate. The posterior margin of the caudal fin is thus subject to an individual variation with regard to contour, and cannot consequently be employed as specific character.

It will hereof be seen that the American «*C. hexacornis*» cannot be distinguished from the European *C. quadricornis* by the characters which Jordan and Evermann ₁state, and about whose value they are themselves doubtful.

In the subjoint table (p. 234) I give a survey of some measurements of the 16 specimens in question from East-Greenland, partly for use for further comparison with Fourhorned Cottus of other seas, partly for the elucidation of the more important differences with regard to sex and age.

The relative length of the head, the upper and lower jaw, the distance of the first dorsal fin from the end of the snout, the distance between the dorsal fins and the length along the

---

[1] l. c. p. 147.

[2]) In one 236 mm. long male, we see the peculiar circumstance that the posterior margin of the caudal fin is sinuate, the middle ray is the longest, two rays above and underneath it are somewhat shorter, the two rays at each corner again are a little longer than these.

(in % of total length)	Hurry Inlet 3.8.1900	Hurry Inlet 7.-8.8.1900.	Hurry Inlet 3.8.1900.	Hurry Inlet 3.8.1900.	Turner Sund 25.7.1900	Sabine Ö 12.7.1900	Hurry Inlet 7.-8.8.1900.	Hurry Inlet 7.-8.8.1900.	Turner Sund 25.7.1900 ♂	Turner Sund 25.7.1900 ♀	Hekla Havn 20.8.1891. ♂	Hurry Inlet 1.8.1900. ♂	Hurry Inlet 3.8.1900. ♀	Hurry Inlet 3.8.1900. ♀	Hurry Inlet 3.8.1900. ♂	Hurry Inlet 3.8.1900. ♂
Total length in mm	68	74	76	93	113	116	122	157	179	181	203	210	219	234	236	249
Length of head	28.7	27	28.3	27.6	26.6	27.6	28.7	27.7	28.5	28.7	28.8	28.6	28.8	27.6	27.5	27.1
" " upper jaw	10.3	10.1	10.3	9.7	9.7	10.3	11.1	10.8	11.3	11.7	11.1	11.1	11	11.2	11	10.8
" " lower "	13.3	13.3	13.3	14	13.3	13.8	14.3	13.7	14.3	14.5	14.3	14	14.6	13.9	14.3	14.1
Horizontal diameter of eye	5.5	5.1	4.9	4.5	4.9	5.2	4.9	4.1	4.2	4.3	4.4	4.3	4.1	4.1	4	4
Minimum interorbital width of front	3.3	4.1	4.9	3.8	4.4	4.5	4.1	4.1	3.9	3.6	3.8	4.4	3.9	3.5	4.3	4.6
Minimum height of tail	4.4	4.3	4.3	3.8	3.5	3.9	3.7	3.5	3.9	4.4	4.4	3.3	4.1	3.5	3.6	3.6
Length of pectoral fins	22.8	21.6	23	23.7	22.1	22	21.3	22.3	25.2	24.6	26.8	24.3	23.7	21.3	24.6	24.5
Length of ventral fins	10.3	11.1	11.2	12.9	11.5	12.9	13.9	15	16.8	15.5	16.5	17.6	14.9	12.9	18.2	16.7
Distance of 1st dorsal from end of snout	28.4	28	28.3	28.7	28.5	29.5	30.3	28.3	28.5	29.3	29.1	28.6	29.5	30.6	29.3	28.1
Length of 1st dorsal along base	14	15.1	15.8	15.6	13.4	16.4	16.4	16.6	18.3	16.6	17.2	17.1	18.7	16.9	14.8	16.1
Maximum height of 1st dorsal	9.1	8.8	9.2	8.9	8.6	8.2	9	9.6	10.9	8.6	11.3	10.5	8	7.3	10.2	8.8
Distance between the dorsals	5.1	4.7	4.6	3.8	4.9	6.5	5.1	4.1	5.6	6.4	4	4.5	4.7	5.6	4.2	4
Length of 2nd dorsal along base	20.6	18.9	22.4	22.6	19.2	22.4	22.1	23.6	21.8	21	20.5	21.9	21.7	21.6	21.8	20.9
Maximum height of 2nd dorsal	11.8	11.5	15.1	15.6	18.3	17.2	13.3	19.1	25.1	14.9	27.1	23.6	16.4	14.1	24.2	23.5
Distance of anal fin from end of snout	47.4	46.9	47.4	47.8	46.9	49.1	48	47.1	50.6	50.5	52.3	51	52.5	54.2	50	49.4
Length of anal fin along base	22.5	22.3	23.7	23.9	21.2	23	22.3	24.2	23.2	21.3	21.2	23.3	20.1	21.6	21.6	21.7
Maximum height of anal fin	8.5	8.1	8.6	10.2	9.3	9.5	9	10.8	14	9.9	14.5	11.2	9.1	9.8	15.7	12.4

base of the two dorsal fins and the anal fin prove to be un-
influenced by differences in age and sex, but are subject to
greater or less individual variation.

The horizontal diameter of the eye is larger in the young
ones than the minimum interorbital width of the front; in
middle sized specimens the two measurements are about equal;
in adult specimens the interorbital width is a little larger than
the horizontal diameter of the eye.

The anal fin starts farther to the front in the young ones
and young specimens than in the adults, its distance from
the end of the snout being in the former ones 46.9—49.1 %,
in the latter ones 49.4—54.2 % of the total length.

The tail is in quite little young ones (68—76 mm. long) less
slender than in larger young ones and the adults, as its minimum height in the former ones is 4.4—4.2 %, in the latter
ones 3.9—3.8 % of the total length.

The length of the pectoral fins amounts in the young ones
and young specimens to 21.3—23.7 % of the total length, in
the females to 24.6—21.8 % (decreasing with age), in the males
to 24.3—26.8 %. The length of the ventral fins amounts in the
young ones and young specimens to 10.3—15 %, in the females
to 15.5—12.9 %, in the males to 16.5—18.2 %. The height of
the 1st dorsal fin amounts in the young ones and young specimens to 8.2—9.2 % [1]), in the females to 8.6—7.3 %, in the
males to 11.3—8.8 %. The height of the 2nd dorsal fin in young
ones and young specimens amounts to 11.5—17.2 [1]), in the
females to 14.1—16.9 %, in the males to 23.5—27.1 %; the
height of the anal fin in young ones and young specimens
amounts to 8.1—10.2 % [1]) in the females to 9.1—9.9 %, in the
males to 11.2—15.7 %. Thus it holds good with regard to all

---

[1]) Here we do not take into consideration the specimen of 157 mm. which
already distinctly shows male characters, as the height of the 1st dorsal
fin amounts to 9.6 %, the height of the 2nd dorsal fin to 19.1 %, and
the height of the anal fin to 10.8 % of the total length.

the fins that their relative length and height in the females are about the same as they are in the young ones and young specimens, but in the males they are considerably larger; this is especially the case with regard to the height of the 2nd dorsal fin.

The difference of sex is also shown by the rays of 2nd dorsal fin projecting with naked points a good deal beyond the membrane of the fin in the male specimens; the same is also the case though to a less degree with the upper rays of the pectoral fins; but such is not the case in the females. Moreover it shows itself in the greater supply of dermal spines in the fins of the males than in the females. In the males 3—8 of the upper rays of the pectoral fins on the inner-side, 8—11 on the outer side are more or less rough to the touch, in the females only relatively 2—4 and 5—7; in the females only the upper rays of the caudal fin are more or less rough, in the males on the contrary, the lower ones are also often rough; almost all the rays of 2nd dorsal fin are rough (with the exception of the posterior ones of young specimens) yet the roughness generally extends farther in the males than in the females. In the young ones the rays are smooth or only show an intimation of roughness.

In the young ones (68—122 mm. long) the horns on front and occiput are very small, low and smooth. In larger specimens there is a great individual variation. In one female of of 234 mm. they are comparatively not much larger than in the young ones, at any rate not the posterior ones, and their surface is smooth, covered by the skin, only, at the distal end of the ones farthest back we can, by the aid of a pocket lens, see some small asperities projecting. In one female of 219 mm. they are considerably larger, the front ones almost smooth, the posterior ones on the contrary spiny along the upper margin; and finally in one female of only 181 mm. they are comparatively still larger, especially the anterior ones, and both pair spiny-tubercular on the upper side. In one of the males of 179 mm. the horns on front and occiput are rather slightly developed and smooth; in one male of only 157 mm. they are on the contrary somewhat larger with an intimation of asperities; in two males of 203 and 236 mm. they are rather small, but spiny on the upper margin; and finally in two males of 210 and 249 mm. they are very large, either compressed and rough on the upper margin or formed like tubercles, and spiny almost all over the surface. — The rest of the spines on the head are developed in the ordinary way.

The supply of rough osseous tubercles of the skin is rather similar; above the lateral line there is on the posterior part of the tail one row, but on the anterior part of the tail and on the trunk there are two, more or less irregular rows; below the lateral line on the anterior part of the tail is moreover found an area, pointed behind, of similar dermal ossicles.

The genital papilla is very short in both sexes.

Fry of *Cottus quadricornis* has been taken twice in Hurry Inlet (a northern inlet of Scoresby Sund) namely:

3. 8. 1891. Hurry Inlet, the south coast of Jameson Land, just near the beach, in very shallow water. 4 specim. 21.5— 26.5 mm. [1]).

7. 8. 1900. Hurry Inlet, in pools on the beach. 7 specim. 23—27.5 mm.

The fins and likewise the rays are perfectly formed at a length of about 21.5 mm. (fig. 2, plate XI), yet the caudal fin is still continuous with the dorsal and the anal fin by a remnant of the larval fin. Occipital crests and snout spines are distinct,

---

[1]) In Bay's treatise they are mentioned (l. c. p. 52) as young ones of *Cottus scorpius*.

likewise the spines of the preopercular. Fine pigment-specks have begun to amass in the places where distinct dark spots will appear later on.

At a length of 27.5 mm. (fig. 3 a & b, plate XI) the last remnant of the larval fin has disappeared. On the caudal peduncle and below the dorsal fins the pigment forms such dark spots or short transverse bands as are also seen in the adult fishes. The osseous tubercles of the skin have also begun to appear.

In fig. 4, plate XI, a 25 mm. long young one of *Cottus scorpius* L. is represented for comparison with the above described young ones of *Cottus quadricornis*, which as before mentioned (p. 237, the note) were formerly mistaken for the young ones of *C. scorpius*. The great difference between them will easily be perceived. The body is much shorter, more squat. But especially the pigmentation is quite different, and so characteristic that we can thereby immediately distinguish the fry of *C. scorpius*: Across the tail, about between 2nd dorsal fin and the anal fin, is a dark band formed by closely placed stellated chromatophores; this transverse band broadens out somewhat towards the back, and reaches the occiput as a narrow stripe along the base of the foremost dorsal fin. The margin of the preopercular with 4 spines; on the occiput a spine which is bifurcate at the end, behind the eye a smaller spine.

In connection with this I give the representations of young ones of two other arctic and littoral Cottoids viz. *Gymnacanthus tricuspis*, and *Icelus bicornis*.

Fig. 6, plate XI, represents an 18 mm. long young one of *Gymnacanthus tricuspis* Reinh. taken in the harbour of Pröven, West-Greenland [1]). A continuous larval fin is still present, but

---

[1]) The date is not given, but a young one of nearly the same size (19 mm.) was taken July 25th 1898 (at the Island Disko, off Assuk).

rays are developed (D.^{1} 12; D.^{2} 16; A. 18), in the caudal fin yet only on the under side of the urostyle. Dark pigment is deposited along the upper and lower margin of the caudal peduncle and a good way along the base of the anal fin and the posterior dorsal fin, partly also under the anterior dorsal fin; moreover part of the dorsal and anal fins is pigmented, and chromato-phores are also found along the middle line of the side, on the base of the pectoral fins, and on front and parietal region. The preopercular spines are visible; on the occiput neither spines nor keels are found (as is well known they are also missing in the adults).

A young one of *Icelus bicornis* Reinh. (about 21 mm. long) is represented in fig. 5, plate XI. The species will immediately be recognized by the large head with two large protuberances, a smaller one in front, a larger one behind, in which the occipital crests end. The spines on the preoperculum are distinct; among the snout-spines is seen a blunt protuberance produced by the upper prolongation of the intermaxillaries. Fin rays are developed as follows: D.^{1} 9; D.^{2} 18; A. 14; in front of the caudal fin is still found a remnant of the larval fin. Fine pigment-specks have begun to amass in some places as fore-runners for the marble-banded colour pattern which appears later on.

Cottus scorpius Linné.

Tasiusak. 5—19 fms. 14. 5. 1899. 1 specim. (Young, 37.25 mm.).

Tasiusak. 6—10 fms. 27. 5. 1899. 2 specim.

Tasiusak. July 1899. 1 specim.

Tasiusak. In the harbour in quite shallow water. 1901—02. 5 specim.

Tasiusak. Shallow water. 22. 8. 1902. 3 specim.

Tasiusak. 10. 3. 1901. 1 specim.

Angmagsalik. 1892. 5 specim.

Angmagsalik. 10—0 fms. 14—16. 9. 1900. Eel-seine. Numerous specim.

Tiningnekelak. 5—10 fms. 18. 9. 1901. 5 specim. (Young ones, 30—41.5 mm.).

Angmagsivik. ¹/₂—ca. 5 fms. 19. 6. 1902. 3 specim. (Young ones, 39—42.5 mm.).

Kangerdlugsuatsiak. 5. 8. 1899. 4 specim. (Fry, 22—25.5 mm.) [1]).

Turner Sund. 2—0 fms. 25. 7. 1900. Eel-seine. 1 specim.

Hekla Havn. 1891—92. 2 specim.

Hekla Havn. 3—4 fms. 1891—92. 3 specim.

Kap Stewart. 6—3 fms. 21. 8. 1900. Seine. 1 specim. (44.5 mm.).

Hurry Inlet. 7—0 fms. 7—8. 8. 1900. Seine. 1 specim.

Hurry Inlet, near the inmost part of the fjord. 3—0 fms. Eel-seine. 3. 8. 1900. 1 specim.

Hurry Inlet, at the mouth. 50 fms. Beam-trawl. 11. 8. 1900. 1 specim. (44 mm.).

Sabine Ö. 5—3 fms. 12. 7. 1900. Dredge. 2 specim.

In July 1870 it was taken by the Germania-expedition in Clavering Strait (Peters l. c. p. 170, sub nom. *Cottus porosus* C. V.).

According to E. Bay (l. c. p. 52) it was very common in Hekla Havn, both in the harbour itself where it stayed all the year round, and outside it.

C. Kruuse tells me that it is common all the year round in the whole of the Angmagsalik district.

The largest of the specimens before me is a female measuring 284 mm.; the largest male is 232 mm. long.

---

[1]) One of these fry-specimens is mentioned p. 238 and represented in fig. 4, plate XI.

As I intend to give a detailed account of the Greenland Sea-Scorpion in «*Conspectus Faunæ Groenlandicæ*», I shall here only state that the specimens at my disposal by the great number of rays in the fins prove to belong to the arctic form (var. *groenlandica* Lütk.):

	D.¹	D.²	A.	P.
Angmagsalik	10	17	14	18
«	9	17	14	17
»	10	17	14	18
«	10	16	13	16
Tasiusak	10	16	14	17
Turner Sund ...	10	16	13	18
Hurry Inlet	10	17	14	17
Sabine Ö	10	16	13	17
»	10	17	13	17

Artediellus uncinatus Reinhardt.

Pl. XII, fig. 2 a (♂) & fig. 2 b (♀).

Cottus uncinatus Reinhardt, K. D. Vidensk. Selsk. Skr. VI, 1837, p. XLIIII.
Centridermichthys uncinatus Lütken, Vidensk. Meddel. Naturh. Foren. Kbhvn., 1876, p. 379; Collett, The Norwegian North-Atlantic Expedition, Fishes, 1880, p. 29.
Artediellus uncinatus Goode & Bean, Oceanic Ichthyology, 1895, p. 267, fig. 255; Jordan & Evermann, Fishes of North-America, II, 1898, p. 1905.
Artediellus atlanticus Jordan & Evermann, ibid., p. 1906.

Angmagsalik. 10—0 fms. 14—16. 9. 1900. Eel-seine. 1 specim. (57.5 mm.)

Off Sabine Ö. 127 fms. 18. 7. 1891. Swab. 1 specim. (68 mm.).

E. Lönnberg (l. c. p. 13) mentions it among the fishes taken by the Kolthoff-expedition 1900, at the North-eastern Greenland. Dr. L. has by letter communicated to me that it was at 72° 25′ lat. N. 17° 56′ long. W., 300 metres deep, and that numerous specimens were caught.

Professor R. Collett has in the stated place given a detailed and careful description of this Cottoid. I shall however add some remarks about some peculiarities which Collett does not mention, probably because the specimens at his disposal were too young to show them in their full development [1]).

It is well known that in Cottoids the difference of sex will often show itself in the exterior of the fish, now in one way, now in another, or at the same time in several ways (compare Lütken, Vidensk. Medd. Naturh. Foren. Kbhvn. 1876, p. 387). In *Artediellus uncinatus* I have observed a hitherto unknown form for secondary difference of sex [2]). When I examined the numerous specimens which were brought home by the Ingolf-expedition from a trawling in Davis Strait, it caught my attention that while nothing unusual was to be observed in the foremost dorsal fin of some specimens, this fin was in other specimens very high. By the dissection of several specimens I was convinced that the specimens with the high dorsal fin are males, those with the low one females. The smaller the specimens are the less is the difference, but yet it is still perceptible in specimens of 57 mm. Also second dorsal fin is higher in the males than in the females, but the difference is not so conspicuous in large specimens as it is with regard to the foremost dorsal fin. The anal fin is about equally high in both sexes. The two figures in plate XII will illustrate the difference of sex between the largest male (fig. 2 a) and female (fig. 2 b) from the «station» in question. For special comparison I give the following measurements:

---

[1]) It is however remarkable that these circumstances have not been mentioned by other writers who have had adult specimens for examination. From West-Greenland there has f. i. been specimens of up to 100 mm., from the Barents Sea even up to 112 mm.

[2]) [Later addition]. Compare however the description of *Artediellus pacificus* Gllb. in Jordan & Evermann: Fishes of North-America, II, 1898, p. 1907.

	♂	♂	♀	♂	♀	♂	♀
Total length in mm....................	100	77	78	69	69	57	57
The longest ray of 1st dorsal fin in mm.	24	14	6	10	5.5	6.5	5
» » » » 2nd » » » »	20	14.5	9.5	12	9	9.5	7

It will be seen from this that the first dorsal fin is always somewhat lower in the females than the 2nd dorsal fin; its height
is equal to the length of the snout (reckoned to the anterior
margin of the eye). In the males on the contrary the difference
between the height of the two fins diminishes as they get
older (in the three smallest ones from 3—2—0.5 mm.), and in the
largest male D.^{1} is even 4 mm. higher than D.^{x}, though D.^{2} at
the same time has increased proportionately more in height
than in the females. The length of the longest ray in D.^{1} is
in the male of 100 mm. equal to the distance between the end
of the snout and the upper incision of the gill-opening; in the
male of 77 mm. equal to the distance between the same point
and the posterior border of the orbit; in the male of 69 mm.
and of 57 mm. equal to the distance between the end of the
snout and respectively the posterior margin of the pupil and
the anterior margin of the eye.

There is also a great difference with regard to colour
pattern between males and females, especially in large specimens.
The before mentioned 100 mm. long male may serve as type
for the final colour of the male sex. The trunk is very dark,
chocolate coloured, with the exception of the belly which has
kept a yellowish colour though with a dark tinge here and there.
On this dark back-ground small white spots appear especially
along and below the lateral line; also on gill cover and cheek
a few white spots are seen. The fins have likewise turned
dark almost soot-coloured with light stripes and spots. Along
the rays the dorsal fins are ornamented with eye-like spots
formed by a white centre and a dark ring; the anal fin has
slanting stripes of a pure white colour; the light transverse
stripes of the caudal fin and the pectoral fins are partly broken

up into little spots which at the base of the fins are of a pure
white colour, but become darker farther out; even on the
ventral fins a single or a few white spots are seen[1]). The
smaller the males are, the more they resemble the females with
regard to colour. The brown colour which by aid of a pocket-
lens is seen to arise from a compact crowding of chromatophores is paler, so that the three characteristic dark transverse
bands can appear, and the white spots are less shiny; still at
a total length of 57 mm. the white pattern of the fins is yet
purer in the males than in the females and is partly broken
up into rounded spots.

The full grown male is not inferior to the males of the
Callionymus-species with regard to height and splendid pattern
of dorsal fins.

The urogenital papilla is not on the whole very conspicuous
in this Cottoid, but yet perceptibly longer in the male than in
the female; in the two specimens of 77 and 78 mm. the length
of the papilla is respectively 1.5 ($\male$) and 0.75 mm. ($\female$).

The males seem contrary to other Cottoids to be a little
larger than the females; from the above mentioned trawling of
the Ingolf-expedition we have 4 males of respectively 100, 94,
90 and 89 mm. while the largest female only measured 78 mm.
The largest female that I have seen is 85 mm.

As will be seen by the synonymy-list I have included in
this species the *Artediellus atlanticus*, classified as a separate
species by Jordan & Evermann. After an examination of
one single American specimen these writers find that it has:
«A blunt occipital ridge or spine» while Collett's figure shows:
«Occiput with a bony protuberance on each side provided

---

[1]) This description is given from the specimen preserved in spirits. Fig. 9
in plate IV in the account of the ichthyological results of the Ingolf-
expedition will give a notion with regard to the colours of the live
specimen, with respect to an exact representation of the mutual proportions of the parts of the body this figure leaves not a little to be
sired.

with radiating ridges», and consequently the American form
which had hitherto been identified with *A. uncinatus* should be
«apparently distinct». If however J. & E. had extended their
examination to a few more specimens they would have discovered
that the specimens vary greatly with respect to the appearance
of the occipital spines, a fact of which I have been made certain
from the European-Greenland material at my disposal. The occipital protuberances are sometimes comparatively high with rather
upright or backwards bent points, sometimes they are lower
and more stubby, sometimes quite disappearing so that no
separation of species can reasonably be based on this «character».
I have not seen any specimen provided with radiating ridges
on the occipital protuberance, nor does Collett mention such
a sculpture, but mentions them in just the same expressions
as J. & E. viz: «two blunt obtuse protuberances on the occiput».
I suppose the artist has represented in a somewhat exagge-
rated way the indistinct folds which are sometimes seen in the
skin covering the spine, so that it looks as if the spine itself
were provided with keels. Finally I shall here state that in
two American specimens which our museum has obtained from
the «Smithsonian Institution» the occipital protuberances are
not less projecting than in many European-Greenland specimens.

Icelus bicornis Reinhardt.

Cottus bicornis Reinhardt, Overs. Kgl. D. Vidensk. Selsk. Forh. 1839, p. 9.
Icelus hamatus Kröyer, Naturh. Tidsskr. II, 1, 1845, p. 253; Lütken,
Vidensk. Meddel. Naturh. Foren. Kbhvn. 1876, p. 380; Collett, The Norwegian
North-Atlantic Expedition, Fishes, 1880, p. 34, Pl. I, Fig. 8; Smitt, Skandi-
naviens Fiskar, I, 1892, p. 167, Fig. 51.

Tasiusak.   30—50 fms.   22. 8. 1902.   1 specim.
Angmagsalik.   10—0 fms.   14—16. 9. 1900.   Eel-seine.
25 specim.
Hekla Havn.   5—10 fms.   1891—92.   Dredge.   3 specim.

The coast of Gaaseland. 5—10 fms. 1891—92. Dredge. 1 specim.

Kap Tobin. 57 fms. 21. 8. 1900. Beam-trawl. 2 specim.

Hurry Inlet, at the mouth. 50 fms. 11. 8. 1900. Beam-trawl. 3 specim.

Forsblads Fjord, at the mouth. 14—3 fms. 28. 8. 1900. Eel-seine. 1 specim.

Forsblads Fjord. 90—50 fms. 30. 8. 1900. Beam-trawl. 5 specim.

Forsblads Fjord. About 50 fms. 28. 8. 1900. Dredge. 1 specim.

Two specimens were taken by the German Germania-expedition in Germania Havn in Sabine Ö, October 29th 1869, at about 2 fathoms (Peters l. c. p. 171). Lönnberg (l. c. p. 13) mentions it among the fishes taken by the Kolthoff-expedition 1900, at the North-eastern Greenland.

In the specimens before me the scale-spines of the lateral line vary with regard to extension; in some specimens they stop on a level with the posterior end of the dorsal fin (or a little before), in others they reach more or less near to the base of the caudal fin. Osseous tubercles are not found in any specimen at the base of the anal fin. The numbers of rays are: $D.^1$ 8—9; $D.^2$ 18—20; A. 13—16; P. 17—19. The largest female measures 75 mm., the largest male 60 mm.

A female 75 mm. long caught at Kap Tobin, Aug. 21st, has in its ovaries about 130 immature eggs, measuring 2 mm. in diameter.

As is well known the male of this species has a highly developed urogenital papilla. Professor F. A. Smitt (l. c.) thinks moreover to have observed this secondary difference in sex that while the females have only one pair of occipital spines, namely the ones in which the parietal crests end, a protuberance or jag is moreover generally developed on the front of

these crests in the males. In all the specimens I have examined from Greenland to the Kara-Sea, a small protuberance
is found on the parietal-crest in front of the large one, whether
the specimen is a female or a male; the smaller protuberance
displays (as is also the case with the larger one) a different
degree of development, but it cannot on the whole be said to
be stronger in the males than in the females.

A young one of this fish is represented in fig. 5, plate XI,
and mentioned p. 239.

Note to the Synonymy. I have adopted the less current specific
name: *bicornis* for the following reason. In the above mentioned place
Lütken writes that though he himself does not doubt that Reinhardt's
insufficiently described *Cottus bicornis* is the same species as Kröyer's
Icelus hamatus, the former specific name ought not to have the preference
because it has not been possible to find Reinhardt's original specimen in the
museum here. With regard to this L. is right in so far as the specimen
from 1838 can no longer be pointed out. But in Reinhardt's notes from the
year 1841, kept at the museum, I find mentioned still 3 specimens of *Cottus
bicornis* sent here from the missionary Jörgensen at Julianehaab; these
specimens are still kept in the museum, and have in the course of time
been relabelled *Icelus hamatus* Kr. As there is now no more room for doubt,
we ought to return to Reinhardt's specific name as being the older one.

Triglops pingelii Reinhardt.

Angmagsalik. 10—0 fms. 14—16. 9. 1900. Eel-seine.
63 specim.

Turner Sund. 2—0 fms. 25. 7. 1900. Eel-seine. 6 specim.

Hurry Inlet. 7—0 fms. 7—8. 8. 1900. Eel-seine. 8 specim.

Forsblads Fjord, at the mouth. 14—3 fms. 28. 8. 1900.
Eel-seine. 5 specim.

S. E. of Sabine Ö. 110 fms. 10. 7. 1900. Dredge. 1 specim.

Lönnberg (l.c. p. 13) mentions it among the fishes, caught
by the Kolthoff-expedition at the North-eastern Greenland.

The species attains a considerable size at East-Greenland,
the largest female measuring 152 mm., the largest male 105 mm.

The spawning-season is late, for adult females caught on Sept. 15th at Angmagsalik, still carried immature eggs measuring 2—2.8 mm. in diameter; the total number of eggs in a spawner amounts to about 400.

The numbers of fin-rays in 10 specimens are: D. 34—37 (D.[1] 11—12; D.[2] 23—26); A. 23—27; P. 17—18; V. 1 + 3.

Gasterosteidæ.

Gasterosteus aculeatus Linné.

Tasiusak. In a pond near Nord Fjord. 10. 7. 1902. 7 specim.

Angmagsalik. In a fresh-water lake. 1892. 2 specim.

Kap Dan Öer (by Angmagsalik). In a lake. 18. 6. 1899. 10 specim.

Danmark Ö. In a fresh-water lake. 24. 8. 1891 & 31. 7. 1892. 11 specim.

C. Kruuse saw on Aug. 13th 1902 numerous specimens in a pool at Kordlortok (near Tasiusak).

On July 31st 1892 it was seen by Bay (l. c. p. 54) in large shoals in Danmark Ö, in quite shallow water.

All the specimens before me belong to the variety gymnurus («Gasterosteus gymnurus» Cuv. Val. = «G. dimidiatus» Reinhardt), as they have only a few laminæ behind the ascending osseous plates of the pelvis, generally 2, sometimes 1, rarely 3 or 4. It is also proved here that the almost naked Stickleback is a fresh-water form. — One specimen has 4 dorsal spines.

Of the 19 specimens from the neighbourhood of Angmagsalik none is longer than 59 mm.; of the 11 specimens from Danmark Ö the largest is only 47 mm. Thus the Three-spined Stickleback does not seem to become nearly so large on the East-coast of Greenland as on the West-coast where the average length for adult specimens is 60—70 mm., and the maximum length 98 mm.

Discoboli.

Cyclopterus lumpus Linné.

G. Holm mentions «Lump-sucker» among the fishes which are found at Angmagsalik (l. c. p. 54), and the same thing was told Søren Jensen during his stay at Angmagsalik 1900. More-over mag. sc. C. Kruuse who has lately returned after a year's stay at Angmagsalik, tells me that our ordinary Lump-sucker is found there, though very rarely; he had however not seen it him-self, but both Mr. J. Petersen (Commercial-manager), and the natives had described it so minutely that no doubt was possible. They stated that the length of it is somewhat over one foot.

Dr. O. Nordenskiöld, who was the geologist of the Amdrup-Hartz expedition, found on August 26th 1900 by Fleming Inlet a well preserved skin of a Lump-sucker about 270 mm. long which had drifted ashore. The specimen has not been dried, as skin and fins are perfectly fresh. Eyes and jaws are taken away, likewise the contents of the head, and of the front part of the body both the soft parts and skeleton are missing. It looks as if a bird had pecked out eyes and jaws, and drawn out the contents through the holes produced in this way. This specimen has been a perfectly typical one, with the following numbers of rays: D.[2] $1 + 10$; A. $1 + 10$; P. 20.

The Kolthoff-expedition found a dead *C. lumpus* on the shore of Mackenzie Bay (north of Franz Joseph's Fjord) on Aug. 9th 1900 (Kolthoff: Till Spetsbergen och Nordöstra Grön-land, Stockholm 1901, p. 163)[1]).

---

[1]) Kolthoff adds: «another specimen is said to have been seen swimming round the ship», but as a certain identification is wanting I do not take this into consideration.

According to Lönnberg (l. c. p. 13) it was the skin of a comparatively large specimen.

The finding of the two last named fishes seems to me to be very strange, nay almost inexplicable, as *C. lumpus* has not been known by any high-arctic coast up till the present time. As in both cases we have to do with dead specimens, the most cautious proceeding will be for the present time to suppose that the animals have been carried hither by transport, f. i. by currents or in other ways.

On the contrary it is a fact that *C. lumpus* lives at the South-eastern Greenland.

Cyclopterus (Eumicrotremus) spinosus O. F. Müller.

Tasiusak. From the stomach of a Seal. July 1902. 1 specim. 86 mm.

Tasiusak. Shallow-water. 22. 8. 1902. 1 specim. 90 mm.

Angmagsalik. 10—0 fms. 16. 9. 1900. Eel-seine. 2 specim. 96.5—103 mm.

Angmagsalik. On the ice near a current. 5. 2. 1901. 1 specim. 96 mm.

Sermilik Fjord by Angmagsalik. 1901. 1 specim. 57 mm.

Amitsuarsik. 14. 8. 1902. 1 specim. 56 mm.

Fry:

Tasiusak. 5—19 fms. 14. 5. 1899. 6 specim. 11.25, 13, 17.25, 18, 20, 25 mm.

Angmagsalik. 9—0 fms. 14. 9. 1900. Eel-seine. 2 specim. 18, 18.25 mm.

Kap Dan. 10—15 fms. 17. 6. 1898. 1 specim. 22.5 mm.

Hekla Havn. 10 fms. 13. 5. 1892. Dredge. 1 specim. 15.5 mm.

Danmark O, at the station. 26—28. 7. 1892. Dredge. 2 specim. 10.75, 13.5 mm.

«East-Greenland». 1891—92. 2 specim. 12.75, 20 mm.

Lönnberg (l. c. p. 13) mentions it among the fishes caught by the Kolthoff-expedition 1900 at the North-eastern Greenland.

According to verbal information of C. Kruuse, it is not uncommon in the Laminaria region in the Angmagsalik district.

In the two adult well preserved specimens from Angmagsalik the fins contain the following numbers of rays: $D.^1$ 6,; $D.^2$ 11; A. 11; C. 11; P. 24.

No great irregularity is observed in the 14 fry-specimens before me with regard to the appearance of the spines: In the smallest specimen (10.75 mm. long) we can scarcely even by the aid of a strong pocket-lens discover any trace of spines, in the specimen of 11.25 mm. length we see on the contrary on the occiput and the foremost part of the back indistinct traces of spines; the number and size of the spines now increase somewhat proportionally to the age, and at a total length of 20—22.5 mm. many spines are visible both on head, trunk and tail.

Liparis liparis Linné.

Cyclopterus liparis Linné, Syst. Nat. ed. 12, T. I, 1766, p. 414; Fabricius, Fauna groenl., 1780, p. 95.

Liparis tunicata Reinhardt, Overs. K. D. Vidensk. Selsk. Forh. 1835—36, p. 111.

Liparis lineatus Collett, Chria. Vidensk. Selsk. Forhandl. 1879, No. 1, p. 41.

Tasiusak. 10. 3. 1901. 2 specim.

Tasiusak. Shallow water. 22. 8. 1902. 1 specim.

The largest of these specimens is 107 mm. long.

By comparison with a specimen of *Lip. liparis* L. (*L. lineatus* Lepechin) from the northern Norway, which I have been able to examine through the kindness of Prof. R. Collett, I have been able to make sure that the Greenland species *Lip. tunicata* Reinh. is identical with this European species. On the other hand I do not feel sure that the Baltic form «*L. barbatus* Ekström» can without hesitation be classified as belonging to the same species.

About the relationship between *Lip. liparis* L. and *L. fabricii* Kr. see the latter species.

Liparis fabricii Kröyer.

Liparis fabricii Kröyer, in Galmard: Voyages en Scandinavie etc., Zoologie, Atlas, Poissons, Pl. 8, fig. 2 (1845); Naturh. Tidsskr. 2 R., II, 1849, p. 274; Lütken, Dijmphna-Togtets zool.-bot. Udbytte, 1886, p. 146, Tab. 15, Fig. 4—5.

Tasiusak. From the stomach of a Seal. Aug. 1902. 1 specim.

Tasiusak. 10—25 fms. 30. 9. 1899. 1 specim.

Tasiusak. 10. 3. 1901. 1 specim.

Angmagsalik. 9—0 fms. 14. 9. 1900. Eel-seine. 1 specim.

Ödesund. 5—15 fms. 6. 8. 1899. 1 specim.

Turner Sund. 2—0 fms. 25—26. 7. 1900. Eel-seine. 3 specim.

Turner Sund. 3 fms. 23. 7. 1900. 1 specim.

Turner Sund. 8 fms. 22. 7. 1900. 1 specim.

Römers Fjord. 120 fms. 26. 7. 1900. Beam-trawl. 2 specim.

Hekla Havn. 1. 3. 1892. 1 specim.

Hurry Inlet, the coast of Jameson Land. 7—0 fms. 7. 8. 1900. Eel-seine. 3 specim.

Hurry Inlet, the mouth. 50 fms. 11. 8. 1900. Beam-trawl. 7 specim.

Kap Hope. 120 fms. 21. 8. 1900. Beam-trawl. 1 specim.

Kap Borlase Warren. 10 fms. 14. 7. 1900. 1 specim.

The largest of the specimens in question is 155 mm. long [1]).

E. Lönnberg mentions (l. c p. 13) *L. fabricii* amongst the
fishes which were caught by the Kolthoff-expedition 1900, at
the North-eastern Greenland. I suppose it is also this species
which was caught by the Germania-expedition 1869, at Jackson-,
Sabine- and Shannon Ö, and which is mentioned by Peters
(l. c. p. 171) under the name «*Liparis gelatinosus* Pallas».

About ten years ago Professor F. A. Smitt united into one
species the hitherto as two species considered *L. lineatus* Lep.
and *L. fabricii* Kr., and designated them respectively *L. (Cyclogaster) liparis* L. forma *microps*. and *L. (C.) liparis* L. forma
megalops [2]). Dr. E. Lönnberg and Prof. N. Knipowitsch
who know the arctic fishes so very well have later on adopted
this view as they enter *L. fabricii* as *L. (C.) liparis* L. subsp.
fabricii [3]) or *L. (C.) liparis* L. var. *fabricii* Kr. [4]). And lately
an undisputed authority with regard to the northern Ichthyology,
Prof. R. Collett, concurs in Smitt's view [5]).

When I have nevertheless retained *L. liparis* L. (= *L. lineatus* Lep. = *L. tunicata* Reinh.) and *L. fabricii* Kr. in the
present list as separate species, the reason is that during the
examination of a great number of specimens I have in no case

[1]) Besides the here mentioned specimens we have moreover a number of
young ones, which I, though with some doubt, classify as belonging to
Liparis fabricii, from the following localities in East-Greenland: Ang-
magsalik, 10—0 fms., 16. 9. 1900. (3 specim., length 42—43.5 mm.); Kap
Dan, 10—15 fms., 4. 6. 1899 (1 specim., length ca. 32.5 mm.); Turner
Sund, 22. 7. 1900 (8 specim., 6—17 mm. long, in Plankton, rapid current).

[2]) F. A. Smitt: Skandinaviens Fiskar, 2 Uppl., 1. D., 1892, p. 287.

[3]) Lönnberg: Fishes from Spitzbergen and King Charles Land; Bih. K.
Sv. Vet.-Akad. Handl. Bd. 24, Afd. IV, No. 9, 1899, p. 15.

[4]) Knipowitsch: Zool. Ergebn. d. Russischen Exped. nach Spitzbergen,
Fische; Ann. Musée Zool. de l'Acad. Imp. d. sciences St. Pétersbourg,
T. VI, 1901, p. 16.

[5]) Collett: Meddelelser om Norges Fiske i Aarene 1884—1901; Chria.
Vidensk. Selsk. Forhandl. No. 1, 1902, p. 83.

been doubtful with regard to species if the specimens in question were not quite small.

Of distinguishing characters two at any rate prove to be «good»: *L. liparis* has a much more lengthened form of body, and a larger head than *L. fabricii*. I have taken 12 specimens[1], 78—207 mm. long, of *L. liparis* for purposes of measurements, and 10 specimens[2] of *L. fabricii*, 75—169 mm. long. The height of the body above the middle of the suctorial disc amounts in *L. liparis* to 14.9—20.2 % of the total length, the length of the head (measured from the end of the snout to the end of the opercular flap) to 21.2—24.6 %. In *L. fabricii* the proportions are relatively 20.5—25.3 % and 25.4—28.6 %[3].

The pectoral fins are also, as has often been mentioned, shorter in *L. liparis* than in *L. fabricii*; their length (reckoned from the place where the fin gets clear of the body) amounts in the former to 14.5—17 %, in the latter to 17—22.5 % of the total length.

The size of the eyes to which had been attached a considerable importance with regard to the separation, is on the contrary subject to great individual variation. To be sure the eyes are as a rule comparatively small in *L. liparis*, their horizontal diameter generally amounting to 2.8—3.8 % of the total length, but it can rise to 4.8 %; and in *L. fabricii* the proportion is generally 4.1—6.7 %, but can sink as low as 3.7 %.

---

[1] 6 from West-Greenland, 2 from East-Greenland, 3 from Iceland, 1 from Norway.

[2] 2 from West-Greenland, 6 from East-Greenland, 1 from the Kara-Sea, 1 from the northern Norway (Porsangerfjord in the East-Finmark; sent to me by Prof. Collett as «*L. liparis*»).

[3] Hereby must however be remembered that these characteristics cannot very well be applied to young specimens; in these the front part of the body is namely comparatively high also in *L. liparis*, and the relative length of the head diminishes in *L. fabricii*, sinks namely (in specimens of ca. 40—47 mm.) to 25.4—25.1 % of the total length.

Other characters, as an ampler (*L. fabricii*) or slighter (*L. liparis*) pigmentation of Peritoneum, are no doubt of too little consequence and too variable to be of any special importance.

This is my impression with regard to the material which has been at my disposal chiefly from West- and East-Greenland. Possibly it will not agree with experiences from other seas.

L. fabricii is evidently a more genuine arctic fish than *L. liparis*. *L. liparis* is by far the more frequent at West-Greenland, from East-Greenland we have only met with it at the southmost part, on the contrary *L. fabricii* is very common in the north.

Liparis (Careproctus) reinhardti Kröyer.

E. Lönnberg mentions (l. c. p. 13, sub nom. «*Cyclogaster gelatinosus*») this species among the fishes caught by the Kolthoff-expedition 1900, at the North-eastern Greenland. By letter Dr. L. kindly communicated to me the following particulars: 3 specimens were caught at the mouth of Franz Joseph Fjord at a depth of 200—300 metres; 1 specim. off Franz Joseph Fjord between Bontekoe Ö and Mackenzie Bugt, where the depth was 250 metres; and 1 specim. at 72° 25' lat. N. 17° 56' long. W. where the depth was 300 metres.

Blenniidæ.

Lumpenus maculatus B. Fries.

Kingak (Angmagsalik Fjord). 25. 6. 1902. 1 specim. 136 mm. Numbers of rays in the fins: D. 59; A. 1 + 37; P. 15.

Lumpenus lampetriformis Walbaum.

Angmagsalik. 10—0 fms. 16. 9. 1900. Eel-seine. 2 specim. 211—223 mm.

Hekla Havn. 25. 2. 1892. Dredge. 1 specim. 174 mm.

Numbers of rays in the fins: D. 72—73; A. 49; P. 14—15.

Lumpenus medius Reinhardt.

Forsblads Fjord, at the mouth. 14—3 fms. 28. 8. 1900. Eel-seine. 1 specim.

The most important measurements of this specimen are as follows:

Total length	53.5	mm.
Length of head	10	»
Distance between end of snout and anus	22	»
Distance of dorsal fin from end of snout	10.2	»
Length of pectoral fin	7	»
Largest height of the body	5.25	»

The colour is yellowish-grey with very indistinct spots on the trunk, tail and dorsal fin.

Zoarcidæ.

Lycodes pallidus Collett [1].

1878. *Lycodes pallidus* Collett, Forh. Vidensk. Selsk. Chria. No. 14, p. 70.

1880. *L. pallidus* Collett, The Norwegian North-Atlantic Expedition, Fishes, p. 110, Pl. III, fig. 26—27.

1901. *L. Vahlii* forma *pallida* Smitt, Bih. K. Sv. Vet.-Akad. Handl. Bd. 27, Afd. IV, No. 4, p. 24 (partim), No. 12 & 14—26.

1901. *L. Vahlii typica* Smitt, ibid., p. 26 (partim), No. 30—39.

1901. *L. reticulatus* forma *frigida* Smitt, ibid., p. 29 (partim), No. 2—9.

This species was caught by the Nathorst-expedition 1899 in Franz Joseph Fjord at a depth of 760 metres (4 specim.), and at 73° 20′ lat. N. 21° 20′ long. W. where the depth was 70 metres (1 specim.). Moreover it was caught by the Kolthoff-expedition 1900 in Mackenzie Bugt (N. of Franz Joseph

---

[1] All the *Lycodinæ* mentioned in this treatise belong to »SvenskaVetenskaps-Akademiens» museum (Stockholm), where I have had the opportunity of examining them — thanks to professor F. A. Smitt's kindness.

Fjord) where the depth was 12—35 metres (numerous [35] specim.), off Mackenzie Bugt where the depth was 100 metres (3 specim.), at the inner part of Myskoxe Fjord (Franz Joseph Fjord) where the depth was 100 metres (2 specim.), at the outer part of Myskoxe Fjord where the depth was 200 metres (1 specim.), at the mouth of Franz Joseph Fjord where the depth was 200—300 metres (4 specim.), off Franz Joseph Fjord (between Bontekoe Ö and Mackenzie Bugt), where the depth was 250 metres (2 specim.), and SE. of Hvalros Ö where the depth was 80—100 metres (1 specim.).

In all no less than 53 specimens were caught in 1899—1900, 40—178 mm. long.

Lycodes eudipleurostictus Jensen.

1880. *Lycodes esmarkii* Collett, The Norwegian North-Atlantic Expedition, Fishes, p. 84 (partim), Pl. II, fig. 19—21.
1901. L. *Vahlii* forma *pallida* Smitt, Bih. K. Sv. Vet.-Akad. Handl. Bd. 27, Afd. IV, No. 4, p. 24 (partim), No. 13.
1901. L. *Vahlii typica* Smitt, Ibid., p. 26 (partim), No. 40—42.
1901. L. *eudipleurostictus* Jensen, Vidensk. Medd. Naturh. Foren. Kbhvn. p. 206.

The body zoarciform. Of the total length the height above anus amounts to $8.1 - 13.6 \, ^o/o$, the length of the head to $19.8 - 24.3 \, ^o/o$, the distance between the end of the snout and anus to $36.7 - 41.4 \, ^o/o$. Hind margin of pectoral fins incised. Colour brown with yellowish-white nuchal spot and 5 — 8 narrow yellowish-white transverse bands. Scales cover the body right to the front of the dorsal fin as well as the vertical fins almost to their margins. Lateral line double, just behind the base of the pectoral fins devided in a mediolateral and a ventral branch, both distinct. App. pyloricæ 2. Size up to 325 mm.

R. br. 6; D. 100—103; A. 88—92; P. 20—22 (23).

2 specimens of this *Lycodes* were caught by the **Nathorst**-expedition 1899 in Franz Joseph Fjord at a depth of 760 metres, and 2 specimens were caught by the **Kolthoff**-expedition 1900, likewise in Franz Joseph Fjord at 200—300 metres' depth. The length is 68—320 mm.

L. eudipleurostictus differs especially by the following characters from *Lycodes esmarkii* Collett with which species it was formerly confounded: The vertical fins have fewer rays; the posterior margin of the pectoral fins have a distinct incision; the two branches of the lateral line are distinct; the colour pattern shows no intimation of the garland pattern so characteristic for *L. esmarkii*; the small intestines have 2 small appendices (which are not found in *L. esmarkii*).

Lycodes reticulatus Reinhardt
var. n. *macrocephalus*.
Pl. XIII, fig. 2 a & b.

1901. *Lycodes reticulatus* forma *reticulata* Smitt, Blh. K. Sv. Vet.-Akad. Handl. Bd. 27, Afd. IV, No. 4, p. 33 (partim), No. 26 & 28—36, Fig. 4—5.
1901. *L. reticulatus* forma *seminuda* Smitt, ibid., p. 31 (partim), No. 13.

The body zoarciform. Of the total-length the height above anus amounts to 10—12.2 %, the length of the head in the males to 26.2—28.6 %, in the females and young specimens to 25—26.6 %, the horizontal diameter of the eye to 4.3—4.8 %, the distance between the end of the snout and anus to 46.2—50.6 %, the length of the pectoral fins to 13—14.4 %. The young ones have dark, and dark edged transverse bands, 7—9, on a light background, besides a dark spot on the end of the caudal fin; a light band across the back of the neck, and on the sides of the head often a dark longitudinal stripe. In the older specimens a more

or less pronounced reticular pattern is developed
through the dark edges of the bands, especially on
the front part of the body. The scales in older
specimens are reaching from a little way behind
the base of the pectoral fins to the end of the
tail, or they stop a little in front of the latter, the
belly and fore part of the back being however
naked; no scales on the fins. Lateral line mediolateral. App. pyloricæ 2. Size: 245 mm.

R. br. 6; D. 91—96; A. 72—78; P. (19) 20—21.

One single specimen of this new variety was for the first
time caught by the Nathorst-expedition 1899, in Franz Joseph
Fjord, at a depth of 100—110 metres. In 1900, 6 specimens
were caught by the Kolthoff-expedition at 72° 25' lat. N.
17° 56' long. W. at a depth of 300 metres, 3 specimens were
caught at 73° 55' lat. N. 19° 20' long. W. at a depth of 150 metres,
and 1 specimen at 74° 35' lat. N. 18° 15' long. W. (SE. of Pen-
dulum Ö), where the depth was 150 metres. The size of these
11 specimens is 61—245 mm.

This variety has a great resemblance to *L. reticulatus* Reinh.
from West-Greenland, especially with regard to colour pattern
as both of them when they grow older have the dark transverse
bands transformed into a more or less pronounced reticular
pattern; moreover they both have a mediolateral lateral line;
nor can they be distinguished by the numbers of rays in the
fins. On the other hand the var. *macrocephalus* seems to be
a comparatively large-headed and large-eyed fish, which will be
seen by the following comparison between two male specimens
of about equal size:

	L. reticulatus	
	forma typica	var. macrocephalus
Total length in mm.	255	245
Length of head .... in % of total length	25.1	28.6
Horizontal diameter of eye • • • • •	3.5	4.3

L. rossi Malmgr. is also closely related to the here mentioned variety, but it has a smaller head (the length of which amounts to 22.4—25.8 % of the total length), and comparatively small eyes (their horizontal diameter amounts to 3.6—4 % of the total-length); moreover it has on the average fewer rays in the pectoral fins viz. (17) 18—19 (20) [1]).

Lycodes seminudus Reinhardt.

1838. *Lycodes seminudus* Reinhardt, Kgl. D. Vidensk. Selsk. Skr. VII, p. 223.
1880. *L. seminudus* Collett, The Norwegian North-Atlantic Expedition, Fishes, p. 113, Pl. IV, Fig. 28.
1901. *L. reticulatus* forma *seminuda* Smitt, Bih. K. Sv. Vet.-Akad. Handl. Bd. 27, Afd. IV, No. 4, p. 31 (partim), No. 14—15, 17—18 & 20—22.

The body zoarciform. Of the total-length the height above anus amounts to 9—10.6 %, the length of the head to 25—28.5 %, the horizontal diameter of the eye to 5.3—3 %, the distance between the end of the snout and anus to 44.6—50.6 %, the length of the pectoral fins to 9.6—11 %. The colour is uniform greyish-brown, or there are indistinct dark transverse bands on trunk and tail, or there are distinct dark transverse bands (7—9), and as a rule a light nuchal band. As a rule the scales stretch to a point above or near anus, rarely to the end of the adpressed pectoral fin. The lateral line is mediolateral. App. pyloricæ 2. Size up to 445 mm.

R. br. 6; D. 91—97; A. 73—78; P. (19) 20—22.

One specimen was caught by the Nathorst-expedition 1899, south of Shannon Ö (74° 52' lat. N. 17° 16' long. W.), at a depth of 350 metres, and 2 specimens in Franz Joseph

---

[1]) Thanks to Professor Collett's kindness I have had the opportunity of examining a whole series of *L. rossi* from Spitsbergen.

Fjord at a depth of 760 metres. 4 specimens were caught by the Kolthoff-expedition 1900, at different places in Franz Joseph Fjord, at 200—300 metres' depth.

The length of these 7 specimens is 129—280 mm. They have all distinct dark transverse bands on trunk and tail, and as a rule light nuchal band.

Lycenchelys kolthoffi n. sp.
Pl. XIII, fig. 1.

1901. *Lycodes Verrillii* Smitt (nec Goode & Bean), Blh. K. Sv. Vet.-Akad. Handl. Bd. 27, Afd. IV, No. 4, p. 22, fig. 1—3.

The body anguilliform. The height above anus amounts to 4.9—5.2 °/o of the total-length. The head, the length of which amounts to 14.3—14.8 °/o of the total-length, is rather broad and flat, the trunk approaching cylindrical, the tail is of a low very lengthened form not much compressed except near the end. The anterior part of the lower-jaw is situated a good way behind the end of the upper-jaw. 7 cavities for the lateral line along the upper-jaw and below the eye. The distance between the end of the snout and anus amounts to 27.8—28.4 °/o of the total-length. The distance of the dorsal fin from the end of the snout amounts to 18.6—18.9 °/o of the total-length. Colour yellowish-white with many brown spots which at the posterior end of the tail ornament both the vertical fins and the body between them, but on the front part of the tail and on the trunk proper they are chiefly found on the dorsal fin, the back and the upper part of the flank; a dark brown spot on the upper part of the axilla, and a dark curved band across the pectoral fin on the membrane between the rays; the upper side of the head brown, its sides and underside whitish; a dark band from the end of the snout to the eye, a dark spot behind the eye and another on the gill-cover. The scales stretch from the end of the tail to the front part of the dorsal fin or a little past this place; the belly and lower part of the side of the trunk (in front of anus) are however naked; no scales on the fins. The lateral line double, rather distinct from the opercular flap till towards anus (the ventral branch), moreover a few pores are seen along the middle-line (the mediolateral branch). App. pyloricæ not developed. The size (of the two males before me) about 130 mm.

R. br. 6; D. ca. 124; A. ca. 110; P. 14—15.

Distribution. Northern East-Greenland, ca. 160 fathoms.

The Kolthoff-expedition caught 2 specimens (♂♂) off the East-Coast of the northern Greenland (72° 25' lat. N. 17° 56' long. W.) on July 30th 1900; the depth was 300 metres, the bottom of the sea consisted of stone and sand.

The most important measurements of these specimens are as follows:

		♂	♂
Total-length	in mm.	128.5	131.5
Length of head	» »	19	18.75
Distance between end of snout and anus	» »	36.5	36.5
Height above anus	» »	6.75	6.5
Distance of dorsal fin from end of snout	» »	24.25	24.5
Length of pectoral	» »	14.5	13.5
Length of snout	» »	6.3	6.4
Horizontal diameter of eye	» »	3.25	3.25

The North-American *Lycodes Verrillii* Goode & Bean (Oceanic Ichthyology, 1895, p. 309, fig. 277), with which F. A. Smitt (l. c.) had identified the here mentioned species, is a quite different species as will be seen by the measurements given below of 2 specimens presented by the Smithsonian Institution to the Zoological Museum of Copenhagen.

L. verrillii Goode & Bean:

		♂	♀
Total length .... in mm.		135	138
Length of head .... • •		26	22
Distance between end of snout and anus.. • •		45	44
Height above anus .... • •		7.25	8.5
Distance of dorsal fin from end of snout.. • •		35	32
Length of pectoral..................... • •		12	10.5
Horizontal diameter of eye............... • •		5	5.5

Compared with *L. verrillii* Goode & Bean *L. kolthoffi* has:

The body more slender, as the height above anus amounts to 4.9—5.2 % of the total length (in *L. verrillii* the corresponding numbers are 5.5—6.2 %).

Anus situated more to the front, its distance from the end of the snout amounting to 27.8—28.4 % of the total-length (in *L. verrillii* 31.9—33.3 %).

The head comparatively shorter, its length amounting to 14.3—14.8 % of the total length (in *L. verrillii* 19.3 [in ♀ 16] %).

The dorsal fin starting comparatively farther to the front, as its distance from the end of the snout amounts to 18.6—18.9 % of the total-length (in *L. verrillii* 23.2—25.9 %).

The pectoral fins larger, as their length amounts to 10.3—11.3 % of the total-length (in *L. verrillii* 8.3—8.9 %).

The eyes comparatively smaller, as their horizontal diameter amounts to 2.5 % of the total-length (in *L. verrillii* 3.7—4 %).

Moreover the dark markings form a marble-pattern in *L. kolthoffi*, but in *L. verrillii* regular transverse bands.

L. kolthoffi is much closer related to *L. sarsii* Coll., from which species it is however easily distinguished by its eyes being comparatively a little smaller, its pectoral fins larger, and its dorsal fin starting more to the front; in a 140 mm. long *L. sarsii* ♂, the horizontal diameter of the eye amounts namely to 2.9 % of the total-length, the length of the pectoral fin to 7.9 %, the distance of the dorsal fin from the end of the snout to 22.2 %. Moreover the colour pattern is quite different, in *L. kolthoffi* very spotted, in *L. sarsii* on the contrary more uniform, only with indistinct shadings down the flanks.

Gymnelis viridis Fabricius.

Angmagsalik. 9—0 fms. 14. 9. 1900. Eel-seine. 2 specim. 97, 114.5 mm.

Off Henry Land. ca. 20 fms. 21. 7. 1900. Dredge. 1 specim. 112 mm.

Hekla Havn. 3—6 fms. 20. 8. 1891. 2 specim. 116, 118 mm.

Hekla Havn. 3—9 fms. 9. 8. 1891 & 15. 3. 1892. 3 specim. 83—106 mm.

Hekla Havn. 3—5 fms. 15. 4. 1892. 1 specim. 107 mm.

SE. of Sabine Ö. 110 fms. 10. 7. 1900. Dredge. 1 specim. 82 mm.

Lönnberg (l. c. p. 13) mentions it among the fishes caught by the Kolthoff-expedition 1900, at the North-eastern Greenland.

There are no colour markings in any of the specimens from Hekla Havn. The others on the contrary are ornamented with dark transverse bands; the specimen from Henry Land has moreover no less than four ocelli on the dorsal fin, the two front ones situated above anus, the two posterior ones fully half a head's length behind them; of the specimens from Angmagsalik the larger one has an eye-like spot a little in front of the middle of the whole length of the dorsal fin, and moreover a row of light spots along the base of the fin situated just opposite to the light narrow spaces between the transverse bands; the smaller specimen has two very indistinct eye-like spots in the front part of the fin, and light perpendicular stripes on the fin, opposite to similar but more strongly marked ones on the back of the body which divide the dark transverse bands.

Professor N. Knipowitsch[1]) has lately pointed out that the figure in Collett's work on the fishes of the Norwegian North-Atlantic Expedition (pl. IV, fig. 32) is not quite correct, as the snout (in front of the eye) is too long. In the specimens at my disposal the dorsal fin also as a rule starts farther back than Collett indicates, namely above the space between anus and the end of the pectoral fin, sometimes behind, sometimes in front of the middle of the line which connects these points; only in one specimen the dorsal fin is continued as a low fold to a point above the hindmost third of the pectoral fin, that is, as far to the front as Collett states it in his diagnosis.

Gadidæ.

Gadus callarias Linné.

Graah mentions the common Cod among the fishes which he saw during his stay on the coast of the South-eastern Greenland (l. c. p. 194).

Gadus ogac Richardson.

1836. *Gadus ogac* Richardson, Fauna boreali-americana, p. 246.
1842. *G. ogat* Kröyer, in Gaimard: Voyages en Scandinavie, en Laponie etc., Poissons, Pl. 19.

Graah mentions this species among the fishes which he saw on his voyage along the South-eastern Greenland (l. c. p. 194);

---

[1]) Zool. Ergebnisse d. Russ. Exped. nach Spitzbergen, Fische; Ann. Musée Zool. de l'Acad. Imp. des Sciences St. Pétersbourg, T. VI, 1901, p. 20.

there can scarcely be any doubt with regard to the correctness of the determination, for he makes a distinction between this cod which he calls «Ogak» according to the statement of the Green-landers, and the common cod (*G. callarias*) or «Saraudlik».

G. Holm mentions (l. c. p. 54) «Fjord-Cod» among the fishes which are found at Angmagsalik, adding that the Eskimo only get them when the Crested Seal brings them up to the surface. I have learned by mag. sc. C. Kruuse, that by Fjord-Cod is meant the cod which the Eskimo call «Ûvak», but this is the same as «Ogak», that is *Gadus ogac* Rich. Kruuse did not see it himself during his stay at Angmagsalik, but the Danes there told him the same about it as Holm states.

Gadus saida Lepechin.

Tasiusak. In crevices by the ice-foot, close under shore (steep rock). 12. 5. 1899. 3 specim. 83, 117, 162 mm.

Tasiusak. 5—10 fms. Dredging under the ice. 25. 5. 1899. 1 specim. 130 mm.

Tasiusak. 10. 3. 1901. 3 specim. 49, 111, 117 mm.

Angmagsalik. 9—0 fms. 14. 9. 1900. Eel-seine. 4 specim. 85, 102, 113, 162 mm.

Angmagsalik. 10—0 fms. 16. 9. 1900. Eel-seine. 11 specim. 72.5, 80, 83, 92, 96, 100, 102.5, 105.5, 119, 158, 187 mm.

Turner Sund. 2—0 fms. 25. 7. 1900. Eel-seine. 5 specim. 58.5, 71.5, 86.5, 95.5, 267 mm.

Hekla Havn. 12. 8. 1891. 1 specim. 254 mm.

Hekla Havn. 15. 9. 1891. 2 specim. 110, 132 mm.

Hurry Inlet, the coast of Jameson Land. 7—0 fms. 7. 8. 1900. Eel-seine. 42 specim. 45—74 mm. [1]).

---

[1]) The size of this fry is remarkably fluctuating viz: 45, 46, 46, 47, 47.5, 49, 50, 50.5, 51, 52, 53, 54, 54.5, 55, 55.5, 56, 56.5, 57, 57, 57, 57, 58, 58, 58.5, 58.5, 60, 60.5, 61.5, 61.5, 61.5, 62, 62, 62, 62, 64, 65, 65.5, 67, 67.5, 68, 71, 74 mm. Probably they are all dating from the year before (I-group).

Hurry Inlet, the south coast of Jameson Land. Just near the beach, in very shallow water. 3. 8. 1891. 2 specim. Fry. 13.5—16 mm.

Hurry Inlet. At the surface. 6. 7. 1900. 1 specim. 73.5 mm.

Hurry Inlet. At the surface. 4. 8. 1900. 1 specim. 185 mm.

Hurry Inlet. In a Bow-net. 4. 8. 1900. 1 specim. 223 mm.

Fleming Inlet. 118 fms. 24. 8. 1900. Dredge. 2 specim. ?—77 mm.

Forsblads Fjord. 90—50 fms. 30. 8. 1900. Beam-trawl. 4 specim. 70, 71.5, 82.5, 92.5 mm.

Bay (l. c. p. 54) writes that it was very common in Scoresby Sund.

It was caught by the Germania-expedition at Sabine Ö («*Gadus glacialis* n. sp.» Peters l. c. p. 172).

Lönnberg writes (l. c. p. 13), that it was the most frequent of all the fishes caught by the Kolthoff-expedition 1900, at the North-eastern Greenland.

E. Bay (l. c. p. 54) mentions *Gadus saida* from the field-ice (68° 43' lat. N. 19° 14' long. W.; 75° 30' lat. N. 7° 11' long. W.) and both he and Sören Jensen often observed some small fishes, during their sailing among the field-ice, which they, undoubtedly correctly, supposed to be *G. saida*. Jensen thus writes in his diary (2—6. VII. 1900; ca. $72^{1}/_{2}$—$74^{1}/_{2}$° lat. N. $4^{2}/_{3}$—$6^{1}/_{2}$° long. W.): «Often when we struck against the sheets of ice, a small fish appeared which I suppose to be *Gadus saida*. It was sitting on the ice-foot in the corner between this and the sheet of ice». «These last days where we have been amongst rather compact ice many small fishes have been seen *(Gadus saida)*.» «*Gadus saida* is constantly seen; in the compact ice where the ship has great difficulty in getting on it is frequently seen». Similar observations were made by the Kolthoff-expedition to East-Greenland 1900;

Lönnberg writes (l. c. p. 13): «A very interesting observation was made concerning the habits of the Polar-cod, which was found abundantly swimming the surface of the sea round the drifting içe even in such places where the depth of the ocean was 2000 metres and more». Bay is inclined to believe that *Gadus saida* — at least at a young age — leads a pelagic life. And Lönnberg writes: «It thus leads sometimes a pelagic life». Jensen on the contrary in his diary is of the opinion, that *G. saida* evidently is no pelagic species whatever, no more than the Amphipods (and masses of Diatoms) which are found together with it on the ice-foot; we «have here to do with a peculiar life of shore species which live out here among the sheets of ice».

The three largest ones (223, 254, 267 mm.) of the specimens at my disposal are females, while the largest male only measures 185 mm. In the largest female caught July 25th, the eggs are 0.35 mm. in diameter; in a 187 mm. long female caught Sept. 16th, the diameter of the largest eggs is 0.6 mm.

The numbers of rays in 6 specimens are as follows:

	D.[1]	D.[2]	D.[3]	A.[1]	A.[2]	P.	V.
Angmagsalik	13	15	20	18	20	19	6
»	12	16	20	17	19	19	6
»	13	15	20	18	19	19	6
Turner Sund	13	16	19	19	20	19	6
Hekla Havn	12	18	21	19	21	19	6
Hurry Inlet	14	15	20	18	22	20	6

The fry (of 45 mm. and more) is pigmented on back and flanks with dark cross-formed or stellated chromatophores. In larger young ones the dark chromatophores are sometimes amassed in some places towards the back, and produce an intimation of transverse bands; the distal margins of the dorsal fins and partly also of the anal fins are frequently strongly pigmented.

In fig. 1 a & b, plate XII is represented a young one of the Polar-cod in natural size (45 mm. long). It reminds us about

the fry of *Gadus virens* by the abundant rather equally distri-
buted pigmentation, but the latter has (at a similar total length)
a very marked longitudinal stripe of closely placed chromatophores along the middle-line of the side of the tail. The fry
of the common cod *(Gadus callarias)* also looks quite different
when of the same size: «The colour is grouped in a characteristic way in dark and light spots on the flanks of the trunk
so as to form a chequered pattern» [1]. Moreover the fry of
G. saida is characteristic by the slender form and the large
eyes.

Two post-larval Polar-cods have been caught on Aug. 3rd
1891, in Hurry Inlet at the south-coast of Jameson Land just
near the beach in very shallow water; they were caught there
together with the fry of *Cottus quadricornis* mentioned p. 237.

The smaller of them is represented in fig. 1 a & b, plate XI.
The length is 13.5 mm. The lower jaw runs steeply upwards
and projects in front of the upper jaw when the mouth is shut.
The median fin stretches from the back of the neck round the
tail and does not stop until just in front of anus. The noto-
chord is continued almost to the posterior margin of the fin,
and is not yet bent upwards; rays for the caudal fin are
developed a little in front of its end, both above and below.
Paired fins have appeared. On each side of the back along the
base of the fin-edgings is a pigmented stripe, and a similar one
on the middle part of the tail, along each side of the under part,
moreover dark chromatophores along part of the middle-line
of the side, on the front part of the tail, partly also under the
middle-line and along a line which almost corresponds with the
upper limit of the abdominal cavity. The upper side of the
head behind the eyes is moreover strongly pigmented.

In the young one which was a little larger, ca. 16 mm. long,

---

[1] Compare C. G. Joh. Petersen, Fra den danske biologiske Station, XI,
1902, p. 7, Fig. 1.

one discovers under a strong lens that three dorsal fins and two anal fins are developing in the form of low ridges at the base of the median fin — to this my attention was drawn by Dr. C. G. Joh. Petersen, and I mention it because the specimen was hereby identified as a *Gadus*.

The two last named post-larval specimens evidently are from this year (0-group); concerning the young ones from the year before, compare the note p. 266—67.

Brosmius brosme Ascanius.

A female specimen ca. 600 mm. long of the Torsk was brought home by the East-Greenland expedition 1900; it was presented to the expedition by J. Petersen, commercial manager, Angmagsalik, and was according to his statement taken from the mouth of a Crested Seal (*Cystophora cristata* Erxl.).

It is interesting that the occurrence of the Torsk is hereby proved; for there can now scarcely be any reason to doubt that it also lives at West-Greenland which was already said to be the case by Fabricius (Fauna groenlandica, 1780, p. 149), but later on considered as doubtful by Lütken (Vidensk. Medd. Naturh. Foren. Kbhvn., 1881, p. 255).

Onus reinhardti (Kröyer M. S.) Collett.

1880. *Onos reinhardi* Collett, The Norwegian North-Atlantic Expedition, Fishes, p. 131, Pl. IV, fig. 34.

Mag. sc. C. Kruuse brought home a specimen of this Rockling from Kingak (Angmagsivik) in Angmagsalik Fjord. It was harpooned with arrow by the Greenlanders June 19th 1902, in small inlets on the promontory which forms the Angmagsæt-place (that is the place where the Angmagsæt are caught); compare *Mallotus villosus* p. 275.

The following measurements will show the close accordance

with the measurements given by Collett (l. c. p. 135) for his specimens.

Total-length........................ 251 mm.
Length of head..................... 50 •
Horizontal diameter of eye.......... 8.5 •
Length of snout.................... 15 •
Length of postorbital part of head ... 26.2 •
Height of trunk above anus......... 50 •
From end of snout to 1st dorsal ..... 47 •
      •   »   •   •   • 2nd   •   ..... 76 »
      •   •   •   »   • anus .... 115 •
From anus to end of caudal .... 138 •
Height of caudal peduncle.......... 13.75 •
The interorbital width .... 10.75 •
Length of pectoral .... 36.5 •
      •   • ventral .... 47 •
      •   • 1st ray of 1st dorsal....... 15.5 •

Macruridæ.

Macrurus fabricii Sundevall.

A female specimen 640 mm. long of this deep-sea fish was brought to the surface by a Crested Seal (*Cystophora cristata*) on Sept. 30th 1901, off the mouth of Sermilik close to Orsuluviak S. of Tasiusak. Mag. sc. Chr. Kruuse who wintered that year at Angmagsalik took care of the fish, and brought it to the Zoological Museum here.

Pleuronectidæ.

Hippoglossus (Platysomatichthys) hippoglossoides Walbaum.

Mag. sc. C. Kruuse brought home 3 small specimens (150—220 mm.) from Kingak (Angmagsivik) in Angmagsalik Fjord. They were harpooned with arrow by the Greenlanders on June 19th 1902, in small inlets on the promontory which forms the

Angmagsæt-place (that is the place where the Angmagsæt are caught); compare *Mallotus villosus* p. 275.

G. Holm mentions (l. c. p. 54) Halibut[1]) among the fishes found at Angmagsalik adding that the Eskimo get them when they are brought to the surface by the Crested Seal. I suppose that by «Halibut» is meant this species whose particular name generally is «The small halibut» or «Hellefisk».

Drepanopsetta platessoides Fabricius.

Angmagsalik. 15. 4. 1901. From a Shark's stomach. 2 specim. Ca. 150—210 mm.

The above mentioned specimens were sent home by Sören Nielsen (commercial assistant); they are half way digested, but can with certainty be classified as «Long-Rough Dabs».

Lönnberg (l. c. p. 13) mentions it among the fishes caught by the Kolthoff-expedition 1900, at the North-eastern Greenland. According to a communication by letter from Dr. L. it was caught at 72° 25' lat. N. 17° 56' long. W. at a depth of 300 metres. Only 1 specimen was caught.

Paralepididæ.

Paralepis kröyeri Lütken.

1842. *Paralepis borealis* Kröyer (nec Reinhardt) in Gaimard: Voyages en Scandinavie, en Laponie etc., Poissons, Pl. 16, B, Fig. 1.
1891. *Paralepis kröyeri* Lütken, Vidensk. Medd. Naturh. Foren. Kbhvn. p. 230.

A specimen of this Paralepid about 263 mm. long was found dead, drifting in the water in Sermiligak Fjord N. of Angmagsalik in Sept. 1892. The body is curved and bent so

---

[1]) It is not correct when Bay (l. c. p. 58) writes that according to Captain Holm *Hippoglossus vulgaris* (Fleming) is found at Angmagsalik. Holm uses the more vague expression «Halibut».

that the measurements cannot be exactly stated. The numbers of rays in the fins are as follows: D. 10; A. 31; P. 12; V. 9.

Lütken has (l. c. p. 227—231) given a detailed account of the species, and its relation to *P. borealis* J. H. Reinhardt, with which species Kröyer had confounded it.

Salmonidæ.

Salmo alpinus Linné[1]).

Tasiusak. From a lake with salmon‑river. 1. 8. 1899. 1 specim. (♀). 455 mm.

Tasiusak. From the mouth of the river. Harpooned by Greenlanders. 1901—02. 3 specim. 125—165 mm.

Sieralik. From small rivers. 20. 7. 1902. 1 specim. 50 mm.

Ikerasausak. From small rivers. 30. 6. 1902. 1 specim. 72 mm.

Angmagsalik. From the salmon-river. 11—18. 9. 1900. 5 specim. 350—390 mm.

Hekla Havn. From a river. 11. 8. 1891. 6 specim.

Hurry Inlet. In salmon-net by the shore. 9. 8. 1900. 1 specim. (♀). 590 mm.

Two small specimens (50—120 mm.) were caught (in July) by the Germania-expedition, in a fresh-water lake in Sabine Ö (Peters l. c. p. 174, sub nom. *? Salmo Hoodii* Rich.).

According to verbal communication from C. Kruuse it is common in all rivers of ordinary size in the Angmagsalik district, nay he even saw it in clayey outlets of glacier-streams.

---

[1]) As I intend in •*Conspectus Faunæ Groenlandicæ*• to discuss in detail the whole of our very considerable material of Greenland Salmon, I shall not here enter into any discussion as to whether we can distinguish between one or more sub-species.

At Tasiusak *S. alpinus*, according to Bay (l. c. p. 55—57), migrates in summer from the sea up the rivers and lakes to propagate. When the expedition arrived at Tasiusak towards the middle of Sept. 1892, the migration was still going on, but seemed according to the Greenlanders to have greatly decreased. Yet no less than 25 fishes were caught on the first day (Sept. 12th) in a small net placed by a cataract; they were large fishes, 1—1¼ kilog.; the males especially had splendid colours, and the hook-shaped jaws characteristic for salmons during the time of propagation. Already on the next day only 11 were caught, and during the last part of their stay only a few specimens. Sören Jensen writes in his diary-notes from Tasiusak, that the nets are put out at the end of July; not a few are caught from July to Sept., then the migration stops, and *S. alpinus* winters in the lake; when the ice of the river breaks up it goes to sea again, but it has then become very lean. — On Oct. 2nd 1891, Bay saw a rather large number of *S. alpinus* under the ice of a fresh-water lake in Danmark Ö.

When G. Holm stayed at Angmagsalik (1884—85), the fishing with nets was evidently unknown, for he writes that during the summer «Salmon» is caught in the rivers with a three-branched pitchfork, during the winter through holes in the ice with a harpoon; sometimes they are also caught by the aid of a dam which falls dry at low-water, and is placed at the outlet of a river.

Mallotus villosus O. F. Müller.

Angmagsalik Fjord. 3. 6. 1899. 2 specim. (♂♂, 150 mm.)
Angmagsivik. 19. 6. 1902. 1 specim. (♀, 119 mm.)
Kingorsuak. 29. 7. 1902. 1 specim. (♀, 109 mm.)

The Capelan or «Angmagsak», in plural «Angmagsat» (spoken «Angmagsæt»), as it is called by the Greenlanders, is eagerly

sought for during the spring at Angmagsalik [1]). G. Holm writes
about this l. c. p. 82:

«The Angmagsæt are caught during the spring in the last
half of May and June at Kingak in Angmagsalik Fjord. All the
inhabitants flock together in this place, and the tents are spread
on the hilly ground which is still covered by deep snow.

The Angmagsæt are taken out of the water, from the
boats rowed by women, with large cylindriform scoops a little
more than a foot high and broad fastened to a ca. 15 feet long
stake. The scoop is made of two wooden rings between which
are placed ca. 12 bars. These bars are interwoven with fine
seal-skin straps, the bottom is like-wise formed by a net-work
of the same material. From kayaks the Angmagsæt are taken
with spears formed by thin wooden sticks placed closely together.
Every bit of ground on the rocks or on the grass is employed
for the drying of the fish which is then afterwards arranged,
drawn on strings of skin, and rolled up in large bundles to be
kept for winter supply.»

«The spawn of the Angmagsæt together with other spawn
collected among the sea-weeds has a fine taste and is a fa-
vourite dish.

The Angmagsæt generally appear before the winter ice is
broken up in the middle part of the fjord, while it is away both
from the inmost and outmost parts. As all the people winter
farther out at the fjord they get to the Angmagsæt-place by a
combined use of boats, rowed by women, and of sledges.»

C. Kruuse told me that when sailing during the fishing-
season past Kingak, one can see the Angmagsæt sport by
thousands on the surface of the water near land. He never
observed any exceptional mortality among the fishes during or
after spawning time.

---

[1]) All the inhabited district has been named after this fish; Angmagsalik
means namely: «Having Angmagsat».

E. B a y tells (l. c. p. 57) that during the stay of the expedition at Angmagsalik (1892) bundles of dried Angmagsæt were
often seen. On the contrary it was neither seen at Hekla
Havn nor at any other place in or north of Scoresby Sund.

Plagiostomi.

Somniosus microcephalus Bloch & Schneider.

According to H o l m the «Greenland Shark» is very common
at Angmagsalik, and C. K r u u s e tells me that it goes right up
to the inner part of the fjords. B a y writes (l. c. p. 58): «During
the wintering of the R y d e r-expedition in Scoresby Sund (1891
—92) a few were caught near Hekla Havn». He also tells
that a Greenland shark was caught while the ship lay among
the field-ice on July 13th 1891 (75° 6′ lat. N. 10° 29′ long. W.);
according to sealers it is not at all uncommon there.

H o l m writes (l. c. p. 81) that during the winter the catching
of sharks is often of great importance for the Angmagsaliks: «A
large opening in the ice is made, and some old blubber fastened
to a stone is let down into the water. Above this is placed
some seal's flesh from which the blood is slowly running into
the water. The catching takes place when it gets dark, then
the Greenlanders run about on the ice and scream to entice
the sharks to come to the surface. Once there they remain
there quite quietly, and allow themselves to be harpooned. The
catch is often so rich that they stop it on account of the
abundance of the spoil. The women often take part in this
catch».

Plate XI.

Fig. 1 a. Post-larval Polar-cod, *Gadus saida* Lep. August 3, 1891. East-Greenland (Hurry Inlet, the south coast of Jameson Land just near the beach, in very shallow water). P. 269.
- 1 b. The same, dorsal view.
- 2. Young Four-horned Cottus, *Cottus quadricornis* L. August 3, 1891. East-Greenland (Hurry Inlet, the south coast of Jameson Land just near the beach, in very shallow water). P. 237—238.
- 3 a. Young Four-horned Cottus, *Cottus quadricornis* L., somewhat older. August 7, 1900. East-Greenland (Hurry Inlet, in pools on the beach). P. 238.
- 3 b. The same, dorsal view.
- 4. Young Sea-scorpion, *Cottus scorpius* L. var. *groenlandica* Lütk. August 5, 1899. East-Greenland (Kangerdlugsuatsiak). P. 238.
- 5. Young *Icelus bicornis* Reinh. West-Greenland (Egedesminde). P. 239.
- 6. Young *Gymnacanthus tricuspis* Reinh. West-Greenland (The harbour of Pröven). P. 238—239.

The appended line indicates the natural size.

Meddelelser om Grönland XXIX.

1. a.

1. b.

2.

3. a.

3. b.

4.

5.

6.

Th. Bloch del.

T.N. Möller sculp.

Plate XII.

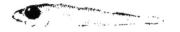

1a   *1b*

2a

2b

Plate XIII.

Fig. 1. *Lycenchelys kolthoffi* n. sp., nat. size. East-Greenland (72° 25' N. 17° 56' W.), 300 metres. P. 261.

- 2 a & b. *Lycodes reticulatus* Reinh. var. n. *macrocephalus*, nat. size. North-eastern Greenland. P. 258.

1

2a

2b

Th. Bloeh del.

Pacht & Crone phototyp.